How
Amazing!

A Prison Testimony

Esther Wang

How Amazing!

A Prison Testimony

Esther Wang

Golden Morning Publishing
Winchester, Virginia

Scripture quotations throughout the text are personal translations from the Chinese Bible by the author.

How Amazing! *A Prison Testimony*
© 1998 Esther Chunyi Wang

Published by *Golden Morning Publishing*
P.O. Box 2697, Winchester, VA 22604

Edited by Leona Choy
Produced by Richard Choy

Library of Congress Cataloging-in-Publication Data

Wang, Esther Chunyi
   How Amazing! A Prison Testimony

ISBN 1-889283-08-8
   1. Non-fiction 2. Christianity 3. Missionary—China—Autoiography

Published in the United States of America

Printed in the USA by

MORRIS PUBLISHING
3212 East Highway 30 • Kearney, NE 68847 • 1-800-650-7888

Contents

The Setting /vii
Preface /viii
Acknowledgments /ix
Dedication /x
Photos /xi
Foreword /xv
Introduction /xvi
1. Great Changes in China /1
     Determined not to leave /1
     God is able to deliver /4
     Wrestling with the Lord /6
2. A Twentieth Century Heroine /14
     Offering water at the risk of life /14
     Presented on the altar /19
3. Abiding with the Lord /22
     Stories of witness and victory /22
     Evangelism and exorcism /25
     Believing in hope /28
     At the Spring conference /31
4. The Way of the Cross /34
     Following him fully /34
     Concentrated indoctrination /41
     Faithful unto death /46
     A thread of light from dawn /48
5. Prison on the Horizon /51
     A voice from heaven /51
     Go out! /58
     Arrested! /60
     A second detention house /66

6. A Criminal in Prison /70
    Sentenced to ten years /70
    In prison /74
    At the gate of death /78
    An evangelistic object lesson /79
    Beaten and punished /82
7. Surging Waves of Evil /89
    My old father /89
    A political accusation meeting /93
    Writing three checks /96
    Observing God's Word /100
8. Prison—A Temple of Prayer /106
    Topics for prayer /106
    A "flying fish" story /112
9. Prepared to Die /120
    A change of guard /120
    God is supreme /122
    Storms morning and night /125
    A presidential visit to China /127
10. Preparing to Leave Prison /131
    Accepting the government's arrangement /131
    In the release group /136
11. Sent to the Labor Camp /139
    Still an anti-revolutionary /139
    "God, deliver me!" /142
    In the production team /144
    "Jesus' daughter" /150
12. At Last! A Short Leave /155
    God's provisions /155
    A precious sister's trials /160
    My treasures were safe /163
13. On the Sick and Aged Team /168
    Sketches of life /168
    Famine for chickens /170

Supporting an anti-reformist /171
Opportunities for witness /174
The full armor of God /176
Exempt from duty /179
Rest and praise /183

14. New Assignments and Trials /193
Plowing /193
Hardship reveals our inner selves /195
Man cannot conquer heaven /198
Satan's tricks /200
Rainbow after the rain /202

15. Truth Will Win /205
My appeal made /205
Off with "the cap!" /209
Living at home /213

16. Blessings Undeserved /219
A motorcycle accident /219
Unexpected visitors /223
Justice to His servants /225
From Marah to Elim /226
Young brother from overseas /230
Cousin from abroad /233
Revised verdict /234
Abundant Grace /236
Prayer and temptation /241
Better house provided /246

17. Showers After the Long Drought /249
A word from the Lord /249
Longing for God's Word /251

Epilogue /255

The Setting

I write this autobiography as the youngest of five children in the Wang family of four girls and one boy. I was born in the city of Liyang in the province of Jiangsu, some 200 or so miles inland from Shanghai.

Father worked in Hangzhou while we made our home in Shanghai. Mother, a Buddhist, enrolled me in a nearby school, not realizing it was a Christian institution. There I accepted the Lord as my Savior. My family moved to Hangzhou where I attended Middle School. At seventeen I dedicated my life to the Lord.

One day in Shanghai I was on my way to Pastor Timothy Dzao's church. The sight of children dying from starvation and exposure on the street moved me so deeply that in 1946 I opened the *Morning Star Orphanage* in the Hongkou district of the city.

The next year I took a Bible course at Prairie Bible Institute in Alberta, Canada. I was prepared to stay longer, but the Lord seemed to be urging me to hurry back to Shanghai. This book is the story of what happened after I returned and endured a seventeen year face-off with an atheistic government while in prison and labor camp. Though frail in body, God, in mighty power, protected and kept me under the prolonged interrogation and suffering.

Esther Chunyi Wang

Preface

Esther Chun-yi Wang is a small, delicate, elderly lady who suffers from several ailments. She dedicated herself to the Lord in her youth and spent her prime years in hardship and persecution, nearly eleven years in prison and seven in "Labor Reform" camp. Many people physically stronger than her stumbled over lighter tribulations, while she stood firm in leading a rejoicing life. Tribulations became a sweet memory, leaving her with the joy of abiding with God.

Sister Wang's life bears clear witness to the glory and power of God and to the amazing experience of those who love Him, proving that "God's power is made perfect in weakness" (2 Corinthians 12:9). Paul's description fits her: "Through glory and dishonor, bad report and good report; genuine, yet regarded as impostors; known, yet regarded as unknown; dying, and yet we live on; beaten, and yet not killed; sorrowful, yet always rejoicing; poor, yet making many rich; having nothing, and yet possessing everything" (2 Corinthians 6:8-10).

My wife learned to serve the Lord in Sister Wang's orphanage so I am acquainted with her life attitudes and experiences for which I have great respect. I am so pleased to know that Sister Wang has recorded her walk in the grace of God. May the Holy Spirit use this to deliver sinners, edify believers, and build up the church. Then God, our Father will be glorified.

Stephen (Yuanlian) Chiu
Fremont, California

Acknowledgments

I am much indebted to several friends who invested their time, energy and much prayer for the publishing of this book.

To Bernice Xia for translating the main part of the book and Mrs. Joyce Kwan for translating supplemental material from Chinese into English.

To brother Kwok who donated the cost of printing the Chinese edition.

To Mr. Ruey and Mrs. Beatrice Chen for their Christian love, support, prayers and recommending the help of Mrs. Kwan. I am especially grateful to Mrs. Leona Choy, an author, editor, and one of the founders of *Ambassadors For Christ, Inc.* Without their help the English edition could not have been published.

Most of all, I acknowledge the Lord's leading and His wonderful blessings to me all these many years. It is His abundant grace and mercy that has kept me safely through all kinds of difficult situations. Not only so, but He is continuing to give me many opportunities to serve Him in different churches until now. I pray that God will use this book to bless every reader.

Dedication

To sister Du Hengwei, who was a faithful worker in the *Morning Star Orphanage* in Shanghai, China. When nearly all missionaries had to leave China in 1951, she insisted on going to Southwest China, to Xining, Qinghai. She faithfully served the Lord in the church of Xining, supporting herself by knitting. She used the offerings which we sent her to repair the church property. In 1958 she was arrested because of her preaching. In 1960 she was put in a cave and killed by a falling stone.

To brother Miao Deqi, a middle school teacher in Sanxi province after graduating from the university. Because of his faith in Jesus Christ and his refusal to criticize the Bible and Christianity he was sent to a village in Kansu where nothing could grow. In 1960, when only twenty-eight years old, he starved to death.

To all the faithful missionaries who were put into labor camps.

To all the Chinese preachers and Christians who stood firmly for their faith in Jesus Christ in spite of many hardships and sufferings.

May the Lord use this book as the voice of these followers of Jesus to all readers.

Esther Chunyi Wang in 1998, Torrance, California

*Teachers at the Morning Star Orphanage
Esther Wang on back row at right. (Chapter 1)*

*Sister Du Hengwei (Chapter 2 and 16) Coworker at the
Orphanage who died a martyr's death in prison.*

Faithful unto death, brother Miao Deqi (Chapter 4)

Mrs. Hsu Lin Yutang, arrested by the Public Security Bureau

Cousin from abroad, Mrs. Wang Chou Che-chin (Chapter 16)

Mrs. Stephen Chiu-Lingli (Chapter 16)

Foreword

Biographies have always interested me. I enjoy them far more than fiction stories. Lives of godly men and women have often stirred my heart and encouraged me in my Christian walk. I was excited to receive a letter from Esther Wang in which she requested that I write a Foreword for her Chinese autobiography, which has now been translated into English.

It is a distinct privilege and joy to recommend her life story for wide reading in the English speaking world. This is indeed a story of triumph of divine grace, enabling her to survive as a witness for our Lord for nearly eighteen years in prison and labor camp. In this way she will continue her witness for our Lord, even after she finishes her earthly pilgrimage.

We covet for this volume an ever-wider circulation. We pray that many young people, both now and in the future, may be challenged by Esther's faithful life and suffering for God to obey the call to serve our Lord. May they in turn experience the faithfulness of our God even as she has. It does indeed appear that we are in the closing years of this great missionary era, and that our Lord may soon return to gather His waiting Bride, the Church, to Himself.

It has been a great privilege both for me and my family to have had some part in preparing that Bride in China.

Paul Bartel

Introduction

Since my release from the labor camp, I have been convinced by the Holy Spirit to believe that "the hand of the Lord will be made known to his servants" (Isaiah 66:14), and that "future generations will be told about the Lord" (Psalm 22:30). Also, many brothers and sisters in Christ have urged me to write my witness to the amazing grace of the Lord.

I feel responsible to share the love and salvation that God has granted me, but at the same time this is difficult for me. I have no wisdom, learning, talent, or qualifications—I have nothing to carry out this important task.

For over seventeen years, more than ten in prison and seven in the labor camp in China, I didn't have the opportunity to read or write as I desired, therefore my vocabulary dwindled. Moreover, I am growing old and ailing like a candle flickering in the wind, so it is not easy to write this personal testimony.

God is able, although I am unable. I have nothing, but He has everything.

By the power of the Holy Spirit, I write my testimony of God's amazing work in spite of my human limitations. I would fail the Lord if He has given me His promise to help me but I do not follow through because of my unbelief. "Without faith, it is impossible to please God" (Hebrews 11:6). Therefore, I dare not disobey God.

The purpose of this book is to remember my brothers and sisters in Christ who have endured tribulation, even sacrificed their lives because of their faith in Jesus Christ and their service to Him. Their faith, love, courage, patience, endurance and loyalty were demonstrated through life and death. They chose to die for the

Lord rather than compromise with evil. What an example for every believer! By faith they still speak, even though dead.

In November 1984, out of love for God and concern for the needs of believers, some brothers and sisters in Christ published this book in Chinese under the title *Amazing!* After much revision, I republish the book under the title *How Amazing!* in a condensed English edition. I pray that it will be used by God's grace, like the twelve stones carried by Joshua from the Jordan to Canaan, to witness to the amazing work of our Wonderful Lord! Thus those in every nation will know that the hand of the Lord is powerful, and people might always have confidence to fear the Lord our God (see Joshua 4:1-7, 19-24).

Praise be to God for this English version. I express my deep appreciation to the editor, Mrs. Leona Choy, and the brothers and sisters in Christ, who, moved by the Holy Spirit, wholeheartedly have supported this ministry by praying, copying and other helps.

I give special thanks to Mr. Yu-Hing Wan, whose left hand and leg no longer function due to a stroke. Despite many difficulties, he willingly took on the task of copying the whole Chinese book to make this project possible. It proves again that God uses the weak. All glory be to the triune God who creates forever and ever.

Esther Chunyi Wang

xvii

Chapter 1

Great Changes in China

Determined not to leave

It was the winter of 1948. Awakened by a pierced ringing disturbing the quiet of the night, I realized it was the telephone. It was Mrs. Chu Baide's daughter. Her mother, my sister in Christ, asked her to notify me that they were leaving Shanghai that very night.

Didn't Mrs. Chu just return from America with me? Why would she leave again in such a hurry? The political situation was radically changing and Mrs. Chu had arranged for a flight to take all her sons and daughters and grandchildren from Shanghai to Xiamen, Fujian. She called to say goodbye. The news of their abrupt departure left me stunned and confused. Since I couldn't see them off at the airport, I bade them farewell over the phone.

During the drastic political changes taking place in China, the Shanghai market was flooded with relief supplies from America. Transactions with American dollars and silver took place all over the city. The value of paper money plunged like a waterfall. Every family scrambled to get food, fuel, clothing, and other necessary commodities.

The city was in a panic, full of rumors. Many fought for tickets to Taiwan and Hong Kong. Huge vessels sailed from the port of Shanghai. The last liner called "Peace" sank due to overloading. Nearly everyone perished, together with their gold, jewelry, and other possessions.

During that period of frantic flight, a plane from Shanghai crashed on its approach to the Hong Kong runway. Despite danger and personal risk, many could not wait to flee to Taiwan and Hong Kong. Some people even escaped alone, leaving their children or parents behind. Everywhere one could see bitter tears, reflecting the sorry plight, while bad news kept pouring in. Meanwhile, people were still hoping for a change of the current political situation.

In the spring of 1949, many were still trying to escape. One day, I heard someone calling my name, announcing "telegram." "Telegram?" Who would be sending me one? The telegram from Mrs. Chu read: "Hurry to leave to Xiamen and take four boys."

Should I take her advice and flee to Xiamen? What should I do about the orphans under my care at the *Morning Star Orphanage?* Where could I send sixty orphans? No, I could not go. Before long, a second telegram arrived, then a third, urging me to leave without delay.

Finally, she wrote to me, enclosing a letter to a senior executive in the Bank of China asking him to arrange cabin seats for me and four older orphans. She would be responsible for our living expenses. I knelt before God, asking Him to guide my way. I felt that I should not rely on wealthy people, but on our forever living God, and that I should not flee with only four children, leaving the other fifty-six orphans behind. Once again I wrote a polite refusal to Mrs. Chu.

For days I felt a constant pain in my right side. It was diagnosed as appendicitis, needing surgery. In the Gospel Hospital, my appendix was removed without charge, by Dr. Qiu Sao Ling, founder of the hospital and a very famous surgeon. His elderly mother, whom I had never met, was concerned about my health. She prepared a lunch of noodles and fresh fish after my surgery. My quiet ward was arranged very comfortably by Dr. Qiu, and I was thoroughly refreshed in body and spirit.

The hospital experience reminds me of something that I always regret. On the second day of my stay in the hospital, staff in the orphanage sent me a note from my former teacher, Miss Woods, telling me that she would have to leave China within a few days. It was not a panic escape; she was reluctant to leave China. However, she was not allowed to stay in the country any longer.

Miss Woods, a New Zealander, dedicated herself to the Lord in her youth. She came to China as a teacher, then God called her to be a full-time minister. She taught God's truth to a group of poor children.

During the Anti-Japanese War, she was the only woman missionary in Hangzhou. An elderly pastor of the *China Inland Mission* and a middle-aged teacher from the *Baptist Mission Board* also remained. Thousands of refugees were protected from being persecuted and raped in their shelters.

Miss Woods led a sacrificial life. With the money saved from her living expenses, she helped poor girls go to school. While in high school, I suffered from a stubborn cyst on my knee and could not walk. She would come to my class daily and carry me to the clinic. There she would clean and dress my wound. When I was working in the refugee shelter, she saved her milk allowance and gave it to me. To tell the poor people in the remote countryside about God's salvation, she braved all sorts of hardship.

How I wished to see her off when she had to leave China! It was a lifelong regret never to see her again. I deeply understood the heaviness of her heart when forced to leave China, like a mother would feel when compelled to leave her children.

God is able to deliver

My resolution to stay in China by faith did not wane. The verse God gave me was: "Our God is able to deliver thee." God fulfilled what He promised me. When all kinds of disasters spread over the city, He led us through safely. The orphanage was kept intact and enabled us to help fellow believers in misery.

After the change of political power in May 1949, I had talked with Mrs. Gordon Dunn, a missionary of the *China Inland Mission,* about their future. Her answer was "God's good soldiers should always be at the front of the battlefield." That meant that they did not intend to leave China. During that time, three newly arrived missionaries from America and Canada, Rev. Donald Rulison, Rev. Wesley Milne, and Rev. Frank C. Wuest, led the orphans to study the Bible and worship God every Sunday afternoon. Not until they found out that the Chinese government would not allow them to stay and continue serving did they leave their ministries in China.

When the missionaries noticed my poor health, they invited me to stay with Rev. Leslie. Lyall for a week. They even invited all the teachers and students of the orphanage to have a feast of noodles in their dining hall while they served the food. After the meal the children played games in their garden. They gave each child a Bible. My present was a gold-edged leather Bible Concordance. It was such a great day that many years later the orphans still recalled their joy.

As I said goodbye to them, Mr. Ben, secretary of the *China Inland Mission*, asked me, "What is your plan? We all intend to leave for Hong Kong." I did not know how to answer him.

When returning from abroad, Rev. Timothy Dzao had asked if I was interested in working in Indonesia. I replied that I did not hear God's call to leave China. Now what should I do, since many well-known pastors and missionaries were leaving? What about the people who had not heard the gospel yet? I was determined to stay.

Then I recalled how Hudson Taylor, the English missionary, loved the Chinese. How could I leave the multitude who had never heard the gospel? The Shepherd left ninety-nine sheep to look for the one lost sheep. Should I not do the same? Then I surrendered: If it is God's will, I must stay in my country even if only one soul was waiting for me to lead him to the Lord. To please the Lord, I submitted myself body and soul to Him and did not leave Shanghai.

Running the orphanage was much more compli-cated under the new political regime. Endless meetings had to be attended and forms filled out. They checked all the books. We had to report incoming and outgoing materials. Much precious time was wasted on trivial details.

We needed a full-time employee to deal with all the paperwork and meetings. Besides, my health was fragile, and I had scant energy to tackle all the red tape. I asked the Board of Directors to appoint a new principal to lighten my many responsibilities.

I began giving piano lessons at the request of some believers. I had an inner feeling that the orphanage could not survive much longer. The number of children was growing day-by-day and they needed more open space, but there was no playground. Also, the boys and girls were growing up and it was very inappropriate for them to live in the same building. The daughter of the owner of the house where the orphanage was located came back to Shanghai from Macao with her family and they urgently needed housing. We were faced with a series of problems.

Some suggested that I close the orphanage and devote more time to evangelism. It was easier said than done. Where would we send the precious orphans? I had no idea how God would solve these problems.

Wrestling with the Lord

When these trials came in succession, Satan also troubled my mind through some distracting affairs which hindered my inner peace and joy and wasted my precious time.

I remembered that in 1949 upon my return from abroad, Pan, a middle-aged man, called me at the orphanage. The man followed Rev. Dzao from the countryside to Shanghai to do literature work in the *Bread of Life Church*. In early 1947, Rev. Dzao intended to move the *Bread of Life*

High School into the orphanage building. Both the owner of the house and I disagreed. The spiritual life of that school was contrary to the Christian faith.

Instead of praying over the issue, Pan took the opportunity to stir up discord between us. I concluded that he was a crafty man. While I was studying in Canada, he sent me pictures to show his friendship. This time he came to ask me to give his wife a teaching job in the orphanage, repeating again and again that "it is God's will."

Actually, it is Satan's strategy to bewilder people of God and trap those who love God and are earnest to serve Him but lack the knowledge of the Bible. Without the help of the Holy Spirit to see through Satan's tricks, one is easily tempted in times of emergency, hardship or haste, to fall into his secret snare.

When Pan urged me to hire his wife, on the grounds that it was God's will, I said: "I have just returned from abroad, so your wife's employment shall be approved by the acting principal of the orphanage." But he persisted in pressuring me. "It is God's will." I believed that God's will on that issue should be revealed to both parties. If I did not receive God's revelation and he claimed that he did, it might not be God's will. At least I could not employ her immediately because the orphanage was still administered by the acting principal.

I learned from that experience that Satan often urges people to act hastily without seeking God's will. He tricks people into believing so-called servants of God. God's work suffers loss and His name is abused.

Pan seemed very pious, but soon showed his true colors. The Chinese saying is true, "Time tells the measure of a man, as travel tests a horse." Pan left the *Bread of Life Church* to teach in a high school. To please the new authorities of the school, he taught evolution to his students and denied the truth that God created the heavens and earth and the first man—Adam.

Can the truth of the Bible be changed because of being attacked, opposed, forsaken, or slandered by some people? No, never! The truth is just like the sun. The sun can be over-shadowed by dark clouds and invisible to us, but it does not mean that the sun no longer exists.

Again, it is Satan working through man. This time he used a different method. Previously, he posed as an angel of light, now he pretended to be an angel at first, then changed into a roaring lion. This time the struggle was much longer than the previous one.

In 1951 there were five teachers besides myself in the orphanage, including a young, high school graduate from Nanjing. He came to Shanghai in 1949 seeking help for advanced education and working opportunity. I considered it my duty to help the poor to get an education, so I provided financial support for him to study in nearby *Suzhou University*, with a teaching position in the orphanage at a monthly salary equal to other staff members.

Another male teacher had been a volunteer in *Hongde Church* after he graduated from the university. Since he had no job, we invited him to teach in the orphanage and take charge of the boys. When he decided to leave, we held a farewell party. Soon he returned saying that he failed to secure a new job, so we let him resume his work.

Since the two male teachers and a female teacher were not well off, I intended to give them the surplus knitting wool in the orphanage as a subsidy. I only mentioned this possibility casually. However, the two teachers thought that tide came in favor with them.

Besides asking for the knitting wool, they demanded that the whole house with all the furniture and materials in it should be at their disposal, thus revealing their inner greed. They seemed to be reasonable people, concerned about the church and earnest in service, but when the chance came for personal benefit, they gave in to their desire.

Should I give in to their greed? Should I let them use what was for the children's benefit for their own interests and satisfy their own desires? No, I should not be unfaithful to God. I should not be unfair to the owner of the house and let down the believers who supported the orphanage for the love of God. Moreover, how could I let the orphans who had been street waifs be hurt again. Such behavior should not be found in a follower of Christ.

At first, they pretended to consult with me politely. When they failed to persuade me, they revealed their true motives by seeking to coerce me. I firmly resisted their attempt. It was acceptable to ask for subsidy because those were times of poverty, but never to seek personal interests by evil means. However, they were reluctant to give up without obtaining certain benefits.

What should I do now? Did not God assure me that "God is able to deliver thee?" Should I fight with these two men in the flesh? No, God would not approve. Because we fight not against flesh and blood but against the spiritual forces of evil in the heavenly realms.

Should I appeal to law at the *Civil Administration Bureau* or overcome them by human power? No, those practices were not from the Lord. It would be a sin against God to take a dispute among Christians before the ungodly.

Since I had no way out, I consulted with Pastor Wang

of the *Bread of Life Church*. But he did not take a clear-cut stand. Therefore, I had no one to support me against them. Should I sit still? No, I knelt before the throne of grace by faith. Like Jacob at the ford of the Jabbok, I would not let the Lord go unless He granted me His deliverance and solution.

Meanwhile, the two teachers attempted to drive a wedge between the children and me, but in vain. That was God's deliverance, the triumph of His mighty power. They searched for a way to discredit me, even searching my personal belongings. Yet they could find nothing that could be used to threaten me.

The financial affairs of the orphanage was managed by an older orphan and a woman teacher. Receipts and stamps were also in their care. Groceries were bought by another older orphan. The account records were open to everyone. Therefore all their efforts to break me down so that they could have their claim were in vain.

When they held a meeting behind my back, trying to stir up the children against me, the eldest among the orphans stood up to fight back every accusation. As a result, they themselves suffered a great loss. The Psalmist says: "The nations have fallen into the pit they have dug; their feet are caught in the net they have hidden" (Psalm 9:15).

I recount these examples to show that my God is truly our Almighty Deliverer. God is faithful and righteous who examines our heart and spirit. Man is doomed to defeat, however deceitful he might be. He may seem to succeed, but he will surely be put to shame. With such a Lord beside me, I will praise and extol His name.

The Lord had delivered me. When it was my turn to lead devotions in the orphanage, God gave led me to share the song, *Leaning on the Everlasting Arms* as my testimony.

When I was besieged by the two self-seeking men,

the future of the orphanage was uncertain. I knelt before my Heavenly Father every day and opened my heart to Him. God said that He is the Father of the fatherless and vindicator of widows. He would not forget the children in the orphanage.

As I sought God's guidance, a director of the orphanage phoned me. He asked if I would consider merging my orphanage with *Bethany Orphanage* in Jiangwan, a suburb of Shanghai. To avoid the intrusion of a gang of street beggars, the principal and the dean of *Bethany Orphanage* were eager that ours be merged with theirs. They knew that we had various kinds of commodities. Our children observed school regulations and were educated and easier to guide than street urchins. Besides, we could meet their requirement—to offer the orphanage of Bethany a subsidy of six months living expenses for each child.

After receiving this message from our director, I called a meeting with the other directors. We all believed it was a deliverance from God. *Bethany Orphanage* was situated in an elegant environment with a garden and a playground for activities. It had spacious housing, and the boys' dormitory was totally separate from the girls'. There was also a chapel for Sunday morning worship.

The owner of our building wrote to inform me that she wanted to give the first floor of the house to her daughter's family, that I could use the whole second floor, and that the ground floor could be used for preaching. I handed the matter over to the Board of Directors. During the discussion, the two male teachers brought up many obstacles against the proposal and the meeting was prolonged far into the night. In the end, one of the directors invited them to have lunch at Kaifu Restaurant the following day.

At lunch, the two teachers were unable to render concrete grounds for opposing the merger, so they asked the director to give them each 1000 yuan (about $500 U.S. dollars at that time). The director could not comply because directors of the orphanage did not accept any financial liability. People donated money to the orphanage when they were moved by God so they could offer no money at all.

Finally, all the directors agreed to merge with *Bethany*, taking no notice of the opposition of the two teachers. Some directors were afraid of being involved. Some were too weak to do anything. I was the only one remaining, a woman weak and incompetent. The only way was to fulfill my duty in the mighty power of the Lord. I submitted the application for merging to the *Civil Administration Bureau* while praying hard for the two teachers. I never doubted God's deliverance in His own time.

On November 7, 1951, God gave me a verse, "Yes, captives will be taken from warriors, and plunder retrieved from the fierce; I will contend with those who contend with you, and your children I will save" (Isaiah 49:25). On November 10, I was still wrestling alone with God and prayed until after one the following morning. That night I received another verse from God, "Be at rest once more, O my soul, for the Lord has been good to you" (Psalm 116:7). God granted me another verse from Psalm 89:22, "No enemy will subject him to tribute; no wicked man will oppress him." Thank God, He did not let me fight in the flesh against Satan and men of sinful nature. He wanted me to wait patiently for His deliverance.

Not long after the Spring Festival, our orphanage merged with *Bethany*. All the children, along with the teachers who were willing to work at *Bethany*, went to Jiangwan. Seeing that all their intrigues were in vain, the two teachers asked Rev. Chao, Pastor of *Hongde Church* to talk with me about their situation.

They each asked for three months salary and a certificate of resignation to certify that their leaving the orphanage was due to divergent views on the merger, not to any inappropriate conduct on their part. In order not to bring shame to the holy name of God, I decided to overcome evil with good and treated them with the love of God. Since what I wrote in the certification would greatly affect their reputation for life and their future, I did what they asked.

About two years later, one of the young men made a special visit to my home and informed me that he was getting married. He also told me that he was working in the Northeast part of the country, that he was hindered by flood and other difficulties on his way back home. I made no response to his hint.

After the merger, some people asked me to work for an educational organization. I refused. I was still looking for an opportunity to serve the Lord, and I was afraid that my spiritual growth would be hindered by a secular job. Besides, my health was very poor.

A Canadian missionary who worked at the *Shanghai Gospel Bookstore* invited me to stay in her house, but for the sake of helping new believers who lived in the neighborhood, I remained in my original residence. Thus God delivered me from difficulty and helped me to start a Gospel Center in the house to continue preaching the gospel.

"Let them give thanks to the Lord for His unfailing love and His wonderful deeds for men" (Psalm 107:21).

Chapter 2

A Twentieth Century Heroine

Offering water at the risk of life

Let me introduce you to Miss Du Hengwei, a co-worker in our orphanage. She was born in Hangzhou, Zhejiang, into a very rich family which observed Taoism. Her father was the founder of "Du Jinshen," the largest silk weaving mill in Hangzhou, which long enjoyed nation-wide fame. He also owned many retail shops which sold factory products, the quality of which won him a high reputation in commercial circles.

Hengwei was converted to Christ while in junior high school. Immediately she dedicated herself to the Lord and tried to live in accordance with the truth as God revealed it to her, despite much persecution from her family. She was often beaten by her father for her faith and driven from the dining room to eat in the kitchen with the servants. However, her faith never changed. Whenever the family was worshiping ancestors, she neither knelt, nor bowed, nor tasted the delicious food sacrificed to them.

After two years of college, she went to work in a bank. Because she wanted to serve the Lord, she resigned and came to work in our orphanage and share the simple life there. Although she was brought up in a wealthy family, she was neither proud nor spoiled. She often visited the poor who were despised, deserted, and suffering from poverty and illness.

After two years in the orphanage, Hengwei entered the *China Theological Seminary* for advanced training. She often said, "We have to go to serve the Lord in the land that God shows us, because it is what God said to Abraham."

In the winter of 1950, she read how David longed for water in the fortress and three mighty men fetched water for him at great risk. (2 Samuel 23) The Holy Spirit reminded her that her Commander, Jesus Christ, was longing for unsaved souls and that He wanted someone to fetch living water and share the truth with them. After much prayer, she understood that God's will for her was to leave Shanghai, the most flourishing city in China, to preach the gospel in remote and frigid Northwest China.

Compelled by the love of the Lord who died on the cross for her, Hengwei resolutely gave up all material comfort, left her friends and relatives, and walked along the rugged winding path of the cross. The Holy Spirit was leading, with all the provisions for her journey.

In the spring of 1951, Hengwei reached Xining, Qinghai, bravely advancing step by step toward the goal destined by the Lord, with firm resolve and a pure heart to suffer for the Lord.

In the beginning of her work in Xining Church, Hengwei was hindered by many difficulties. But she kept onward, never retreating and often going with a brother minister on bicycle to visit believers in remote mountains and deep valleys.

One day they passed many narrow and winding roads and reached a desolate mountain area where some very poor believers lived. In their shabby rooms hung some posters with gospel songs. They told Hengwei how they longed for God to send His servants to teach them the truth. Their hunger for spiritual food greatly strengthened her resolve to serve the Lord in that remote area. She was persistent in her ministry to feed hungry sheep in that deserted, barren land. Even in the most difficult situation, she shared with them God's Living Water and spiritual food.

Not long afterwards, the brother minister was arrested and sent to a labor camp. Hengwei had to shoulder the ever-increasing responsibilities and daily pressures of the church. Some in the congregation were quarrelsome and hurled abuses at her. The minister's wife even unfavorably affected other believers by her smoking and other bad habits. Hengwei felt "a weight as heavy as a rock laid on her heart." Did she lose heart? No, never! Hengwei did not lose her courage, nor did she retreat. Such undaunted faith and perseverance is found only in those filled with the Holy Spirit. She even urged her cousin and younger brother to come and study in Xining, Qinghai, hoping they would form good habits from an early age by leading a simple life there.

During that period, two sister ministers from *Beijing Theological Seminary* came to serve in the church. One had the gift of preaching. They excluded Hengwei and seldom talked with her. They even refused to prepare meals with her, not because they had to keep a special diet, but to purposely create division. Hengwei felt very lonely.

Children of God are to have concern for each other and be open-minded. If two of us are friends and are reluctant to share fellowship with a third or more fellow believers, we cannot glorify God. Instead, we will hinder His ministry.

We are exhorted in Ephesians 4:15-16: ". . . in all things grow up into Him Who is the Head, that is, Christ. From Him the whole body joined and held together by every supporting ligament, grows and builds itself up in love, as each part does its work."

For years, Hengwei led a lonely and poor life with little support from co-workers. Although she was like "a bird alone on a roof" (Psalm 102:7), she firmly believed that the Lord was with her. She preferred to walk with God in the darkness than to be in the light without Him. Humble and gentle, she followed the Holy Spirit by faith, preaching the gospel in all seasons and devoting herself to a ministry which attracted no attention or praise.

One Sunday, as the morning worship was ending, some believers came from a mountain area about 50 miles away, swineherds who migrated from other provinces. It took them a long time to find a church where they could worship God. Their coming filled Hengwei with both joy and grief. She was joyous that even in such a poor and deserted mountain area there were believers who would travel such a long distance to worship God. She was grieved when she thought that those poor believers were like sheep without a shepherd to care for them.

When foreigners were coming to visit the church, the *Religious Affairs Bureau* would instruct Hengwei and other ministers to use any means—to gather as many believers as possible for worship service. Thus, the foreigner visitors would see an excessively large attendance in the church.

By the end of 1956, Hengwei made a visit home. She intended to go home with her cousin, but he refused to go with her because he was ashamed to be on the same bus with a minister. With heavy luggage on her back, she had to walk a long way to catch the bus and then change to a train for Shanghai.

During her stay in Shanghai, she took every opportunity to tell people about God's amazing work in the church of Xining in order to encourage believers there. How amazing . . . her habitual stutter disappeared whenever she talked about God's grace! She was obviously empowered by Almighty God, which proved that she was truly His faithful servant sent to feed His sheep. All glory to God, by whom immeasurable deeds and immeasurable miracles have been done!

Some people returned from Northwest China and never went back because of the hardship and danger in the frontier life. However, Hengwei insisted on going back, although her health had begun to deteriorate. She was thin and suffered badly in cold weather. Besides, some worldly people in the church of Xining tried every means to push her out. They insulted her and made things difficult for her, but nothing shook her resolve to distribute spiritual food to the hungry flock.

Before her return to Xining, she sensed intuitively that there would be tribulation and imprisonment ahead. Several times she mentioned what an elder in Xining said to her: "The Lord will assuredly plant you in this land" (Jeremiah 32:41). Indeed like a green pine braving storm and drought, blazing hot and freezing cold, she stood firmly on the deserted ridge of Xining, bearing witness for the Lord.

Hengwei was honest in her dealings and did not like flattery. Occasionally, when she noticed other people's shortcomings, she would gently tell them face to face. One time she reproved me, saying, "You are often concerned about my physical needs, but not about my spiritual life and ministry. You have so much flannel material for Sunday School, but you do not share any with me." I had considered her spiritual life so vigorous that she did not need my help. As to the flannel materials, she was right to reprove me. Since she did it out of goodwill, I was willing to accept it and confess before God. I prayed that God would remind me of the spiritual need of my brothers and sisters in Christ and that I would not commit the same error in the future.

In her letters, she often mentioned how she longed to be closer to the Lord and to please Him more. Despite her cheerful letters, I was fearful that she might not endure the heavy labor. I asked her sister to send her money for traveling expenses and urged her to come back for a break, but she returned the money.

At that time, her belongings were often searched and she was told that it would be illegal to stay single. However, moved by the mighty power of God, she continued her ministry with faith, love and patience, breaking one barrier after another to send Living Water to thirsty people. She knew that the Lord was pleased by what she did. Indeed, she did everything she could for the Lord.

Presented on the altar

One night in October 1958, I saw Hengwei in a dream. She was very sad, standing still and lonely. I felt that the dream was related to her safety, and that something had happened to her. I became very anxious.

A few days later, my muscles and joints felt sore all over so I went to my physiotherapist. As soon as he saw me, he said that Hengwei's mother wanted me to visit her. Going quickly, I asked her, "Did something happen to

Hengwei?" She asked how did I know. I told her what I saw in my dream a few days ago. Then she told me that her nephew wrote her a letter, telling her that Hengwei, before an assembly of 10,000 people, was dragged onto a platform during a political accusation meeting and attacked.

Some people pulled her hair, spit at her and struck her in the face. Others made up all sorts of bad stories to incriminate her. At the end of the meeting, she was thrown into prison.

The news came suddenly and was totally beyond her mother's perception. Since then we lost track of her. Even her mother did not know where she was.

It made me very sad to lose touch with Hengwei after she was sent to prison. Therefore, before Easter of 1960, I visited her mother in Hangzhou, asking her to write a letter to the *Public Security Bureau* to inquire about Hengwei's whereabouts. But her mother was afraid to do it. Time passed relentlessly. Soon autumn came with its harvest season, and the ground was covered with fallen leaves. Again I had a dream. In my vision, I saw Hengwei looking at me joyfully, beaming with smiles. She seemed to tell me: "Rest assured that I am no longer in bondage. The Lord has received my sacrifice. Now I can be close to the Lord and worship Him forever." Foolishly, I did not realize that the Lord had already taken her to Paradise.

For two years, her mother, brothers and sisters did not hear from her. The letters sent by her elder sister were all returned by the post office. No one heard from any government agency. Then one day a sister in Christ came to see me and told me that Hengwei "was sacrificed on the altar." She was sacrificed! In human terms it meant that she was dead. When and how did she die? Neither her family nor I had any information about it.

You might ask why God did not deliver her since she loved Him so much? Why did He cover His face and not see it? Why did He not listen to the prayers of believers? Did He have no power to deliver? Was He not enforcing justice in her case? Why should He allow her to leave the earth so early?

The answer is very simple: God allowed her life to be taken because she was willing to offer her life as a living sacrifice to the Lord. Her love of God was far more precious to her than her life. God granted her the honor of being a sacrifice for Him.

As it is written: "They overcame him by the blood of the Lamb and by the word of their testimony; they did not love their lives so much as to shrink from death" (Revelation 12:11). Like the saints of faith recorded in Hebrews, she was a heroine.

Dr. A. B. Simpson said this about how the Lord rewards those who love Him: "The Lord does not consider quantity but the deepest, most primitive motive. What Stephen did in one day equals what Barnabas did in his whole life. In the future the most significant requirement for reward from the Lord is not based on the appearance of the work but on the sincerity of loving kindness and the willingness of sacrificing oneself for the sake of the Lord."

I firmly believe that when the Lord, our Savior, comes again, all that Sister Du Hengwei has done will be rewarded with the crown of righteousness which God has in store for all those who love Him.

Chapter 3

Abiding with the Lord

Stories of witness and victory

After merging our orphanage with *Bethany Orphanage*, we converted the ground floor into a Gospel Center. The Lord led sister Shi to come to be in charge of preaching and sister Huang, of visitation. Miss Huang used to work in the *Children's Affair Services* in Hangzhou. After her service in that organization was terminated, someone advised her to come to Shanghai with two other sisters in Christ and train for medical technology. She was unable to complete the training course because of poor health, so I invited her to stay with me. She started her work in the evangelical center after her health improved.

Near the Gospel Center lived a young girl suffering from bone tuberculosis. She was converted im our Sunday School class, but no one else in her family believed in Jesus. She lived with her elder brother who had many children.

Supported by his meager income, the family had nothing left to pay her medical bills.

Day and night the young girl lay on the floor in a small, filthy attic, with no one to care for her. Thus her condition worsened. However, she was renewed inwardly day-by-day through her simple faith in the Lord, and her heart was filled with heavenly peace.

The day before she left this world, she told her mother and brother-in-law, "Tomorrow night at eleven o'clock I am going to my heavenly home. I have already seen it and tasted the delicious fruit there." Just as she predicted, she went happily to see her Heavenly Father at exactly that hour. Amazed by this fulfillment, her mother soon became a follower of Jesus.

There was a time in the country when food was scant and life was hard. One morning about five o'clock the girl's mother came to my house with a piece of pig liver. Quietly she put it on my cabinet and left. Lord, please remember that poor widow and reward her abundantly.

People came to hear witness of God's amazing work in our Gospel Center. A certain country woman who was illiterate, at the moment she was leaving this world quoted this message from Ezekiel 34:16: "I will search for the lost and bring back the strayed. I will bind up the injured and strengthen the weak, but the sleek and the strong I will destroy. I will shepherd the flock with justice." When she finished the verse, she went to her heavenly home. Her husband, not a Christian, witnessed to that later. She rested from her work on earth, but what she did at the end of her life remained as a comfort and a warning to Christians today.

Near the Gospel Center there lived a Mr. Zhang, whose two sons, both medical students, died in an accidental fire at their home. Salvation came to him through that incident. He built a successful undergarment factory. During the political movement, he was falsely accused by his confidential friend, which broke his heart. Satan worked in him and made him feel that it was better to die than to live. With tears in his eyes, he asked me to take care of his three young daughters, ranging in age from five to ten. The only way to solve such a problem was to kneel down with him and ask the Lord to take care of his family and his career. The Lord heard our prayer and encouraged him. When we finished praying, God filled his heart with peace and removed his thoughts of suicide. Revived by the Lord, he returned to his work with joy.

The Chinese government launched a movement in 1951-52 for the purpose of attacking the evil practices of bribery, corruption, and bureaucratism in the various organizations, especially those of the Party, government and army. It continued the following year against tax evasion, fraud, stealing state property, concealing capital estate and theft of economic secrets. It was called The Three Anti's movement. Because of these regulations, Mr. Zhang's factory was pronounced a law-abiding enterprise, and he did not suffer any loss. Later, God gave him three sons and turned his bitterness into joy.

Rev. Timothy Dzao wrote me letters repeatedly inviting me to work abroad. I thought that there were already too many ministers outside the country, and too few remained to take care of the many lost sheep in China. Besides, I was very concerned about the churches in China, so I kept declining his invitations.

At that time the materials published by the Sunday School Board in the country were mingled with political propaganda, not appropriate for teaching God's truth. Someone suggested that I compile some materials in addition to those from the Sunday School Board, a job I accepted quite willingly, with the help of the Holy Spirit. The Gospel Center later adopted these materials.

About twenty years later, I met a young man in the street who told me, "When I was a child, I heard the gospel in your Gospel Center. Later I was faced with an unsolvable problem. I prayed, and God heard my prayer by giving me what I prayed for."

Another young man told a sister in our Gospel Center, "I first heard the gospel in your Center. When I was in difficulty, I knelt down before God and prayed. The Lord heard my prayer and now I am saved by Him."

God's Word says, "Sow your seed in the morning, and at evening let not your hands be idle, for you do not know which will succeed, whether this or that, or whether both will do equally well" (Ecclesiastes 11:6). Indeed the Lord examines the hearts of those who are honest before Him.

Evangelism and exorcism

In the autumn of 1953, we held a revival meeting in the Gospel Center. An emaciated, fatigued, middle-aged man, whose wife suffered from a serious mental disorder, approached me. Dr. Shu Zonghua, the famous psychiatrist, was treating her, but none of the treatments worked. His prognosis: such dementia was incurable.

At home, she would tear her clothes off and refuse to eat. He pleaded to let her stay with me and pray for her. Because I had no experience in healing mental illness by prayer, nor by exorcism, nor had I ever seen such a demonic person before, I dared not promise him anything.

I said, "We shall ask God first. If God permits, she can come. Otherwise, there is no need for her coming." After prayer and reading the Bible, we knew that our Heavenly

Father would show mercy to her, and she moved into our Gospel Center.

Our housing was quite spacious. The woman and her attendant stayed in our living room next to my little bedroom. In the dead of night, she began her endless talking under her quilt, which frightened her companion so much that she left to return home.

In the beginning, her family had her meals sent to our house. Later they stopped sending any food, so she had to eat with us. What should I do under such circumstances? I had no choice but to accompany her. Her behavior was beyond description, but I had to watch her constantly. Every time she saw her husband, she would shout abuses at him in foul language.

Soon after she came, I took her to a worship service. I was so embarrassed to see her dancing down the street that I did not know whether to laugh or cry. She was really possessed by an evil spirit. Supported by the Lord, I prayed for her in silence all the time.

For the love of the Lord, we could do nothing but care for her and ask Him to rescue her. When we prayed for her, she would run to the balcony and strip off her clothes, yelling, "Look, Mr. Pastor is beating me up." She came from a Buddhist family, and her husband was also a devout Buddhist and often published books of Buddhist literature and gave them away.

Since we could do nothing for her, we asked the Lord to bind Satan. Powerful prayer is what Satan fears most, a most powerful spiritual weapon to attack his fortress.

The more the woman hated us praying, the more we persisted in praying with united hearts. Gradually she calmed down. One night, I woke up suddenly and saw an animal like a panda jumping out of our window. After that, the woman no longer fought with me when I took her to bathe.

She would be scared whenever we prayed, saying that she was possessed by three devils from an airplane. I asked her, "What kind of devils?" She answered, "Sinful, unbelieving heart." "Sinful, unbelieving heart" is not a phrase used in Buddhism, but a verse quoted from Hebrews 3:12. That convinced me that Satan was well aware of the spiritual life of a Christian.

One morning, when we were singing "There's wonderful power in the blood of the Lamb" she even said, "magic power." Every time when we asked her to close her eyes to pray, she would say, "Cannot close, cannot close." Many brothers and sisters in Christ came to pray for her, asking the Lord to deliver her quickly.

One day, the Holy Spirit moved me to take her to the Gospel Center where I prayed and fasted for her. After singing a hymn, I lightly touched her eyes in the name of victorious Jesus, the Lord. It was a marvel that she yelled bitterly "Ahyio, Ahyio," appearing in extreme pain. She cried aloud with tears streaming down her face, as if she lost her parents or dearest one.

Since then she became obedient. Quiet and meek, she no longer shouted abuse at her husband when she saw him. Little by little her sanity was restored, and she began to do some drawing and knitting. Eventually she fully recovered, returning to her home a normal woman. Jesus says, "This kind of devil will not go out but by prayer and fasting." Everyone who knew the woman and saw that she was cured by the mighty power of the Lord, rejoiced and marveled at the wonderful work of God.

Mrs. Yeh was the proprietress of a rubber shop. She had been a Christian, but was very weak physically and spiritually. Satan took the chance to work through her. She would grip her children's arms for a long time, which hurt her children and made them all dislike her. Her children would beat her fiercely until her arms were bruised in order to be released from her grip. The condition of her illness was getting worse. In her helplessness, she begged to stay with us, hoping that we would pray for her. After prayer, she gradually got better. In a few days, she fully recovered.

Those experiences showed me once again how God demonstrated His wonderful power on those who believed in Him. Jesus told us, "Do not rejoice that the spirits submit to you, but rejoice that your names are written in heaven" (Luke 10:20). Pray that we will not regard miracles higher than Jesus Christ, and that we will exalt the Lord Himself and the salvation He accomplished for us.

Believing in hope

In the summer of 1956, the mother of one of my students told me that she was going to Japan. I heard a small voice, saying, "You go along with her." But my faith was not strong enough to follow the voice, thinking that I had no acquaintance in Japan and that I would become a burden to others. Besides, I was still concerned about these lost sheep. Who would lead them and feed them? From my heart often came a cry, "Lord, I am willing to stay if I can lead only one person to you." Therefore, I gave no further thought about going to Japan, nor prayed for it.

One day, I was invited to play the music in a memorial service of a blessed old lady who died in her nineties. In the funeral parlor, I met Mother Hsu, the daughter-in-law of the deceased, who hurried back from abroad to attend the funeral. Mother Hsu (Liu Yutang), a sister in Christ, was noted for her faith and kindness. She was eager for the truth after she was converted, and was a regular attender at family gatherings and Bible study classes for new believers when she was in China. I recalled that when her mother-in-law was ill, she requested us to pray for the old lady. Because of her faith, the old lady recovered.

Later she went with her husband to Hong Kong. While there, she often sent money to our orphanage. The property for *Bread of Life Church* in Hong Kong was also bought with her assistance. She was truly enthusiastic about the Lord's work.

Because of the Korean War, her husband's business in Hong Kong suddenly collapsed. Some of the employees were not loyal, and the family fortune was lost. According to Hong Kong law, the wife was not responsible for her husband's debt. However, Mother Hsu took out her private savings to repay the debt for her husband.

While her husband was in despair and the children were dying of hunger, Mother Hsu prayed fervently in faith, waiting with all her heart for grace from her Heavenly Father, who, she firmly believed, would deliver them. As she expected, God strengthened her faith by giving her wisdom to guide her husband out of the dense fog of boundless grief and despair. Because of her prayers, God moved her brother in Japan to invite her family to move to that country and start a business there.

The grace of God is for those who wait for His delivery from their misery. He turns their darkness into light. Praise the Lord that she walked through the valley of the shadow of death and suffered no evil because of her trust in the Lord and her obedience. Like Abraham, she believed in hope against all hope. She did not waver through unbelief. Strengthened in her faith, she gave glory to God.

Once in Japan, Mother Hsu offered her house to the Lord for a meeting place. A sister who knew her told me that she often humbly served the workers of God, even washing their clothes or mending socks. Moreover, she went door-to-door looking for lost sheep. In the face of abuse, she remained gentle and sweet, persistent in preaching the gospel.

This time she could only stay in China briefly. However, she was eager to reach unsaved people. She invited me to share God's truth with a woman she met on her way back to China. When we went to meet that woman, I remembered that there was a piano student waiting for me. So after I finished my sharing, I hurried back home to give the student a piano lesson. But Mother Hsu continued explaining the good news in Christ to the woman. It was like what Jesus said in Matthew 19:30: "Many who are first will be last, and many who are last will be first." At that time, her love for the Lord and eagerness to win unsaved souls for the Lord far surpassed mine. I felt ashamed. O Lord, please have mercy on me, an unfaithful maiden.

Not only did she believe in God, she brought her husband and children to the Lord in the power of the Holy Spirit. I remember she told me once, "I will bring every one of my children to the Lord and let them trust Him and know Him by themselves. One day, we parents will leave them, but the Lord will never leave them."

God satisfied her desire and gave her a very lovely son, who loved the Lord and his neighbors earnestly. He would make the most of his efforts for the ministry of the Lord no matter how busy he was or how difficult the job. He was willing to do all kinds of ministry with no consideration for meals or pay. He told me, "Nothing that you have offered to the Lord is not abundantly rewarded. It is the most valuable thing to pursue."

One day he prayed, "Lord, we came empty-handed from our mother's womb and we can take nothing with us when we die." He tried his best to do whatever ministry was available to him.Once he told his friend, "It is my comfort and joy to do things properly." He not only said that, he did so in practice. Once he brought from abroad several copies of the Bible for the believers in the country. However, the Customs House of China did not allow him to carry so many copies into the country, and he suffered a loss. It almost moved me to tears to see his grievous look.

Dear God, You raise the dead and create from nothing, please deliver the lost souls and feed the hungry and thirsty sheep with the Bread of Life to soothe his mourning heart. May Your wonderful deeds be revealed in China, the vast land where there are still many places that have not been reached by the gospel.

At the Spring conference

God often achieves unexpected things through unexpected people. One day I was invited to hold a New Spring Conference in the countryside. The house used for the gathering was built by an old lady, Mrs. Cai. During the Anti-Japanese War she fled from Wenzhou to that small town far away. Immediately she began to search for a place to worship the Lord. She was so disappointed to find that there was no church that she decided to build one.

Although without learning or wealth, she had faith and love for the Lord. Quietly she put aside one-tenth of her income as the building fund for a church. The Lord received her offering and greatly blessed her. A few years later, God prepared a piece of land for her on which she built a church seating over 400 people.

Every Sunday, crowds of people came to the church by foot and by boat. Some started walking to the church before dawn. They held gatherings all day. At noon they had their lunch in nearby small shops or ate what they brought with them. God confirmed His word by signs and miracles. Many sick and demon-possessed were healed through prayer.

I saw it as an opportunity from the Lord to serve Him. The brother in charge loved the Lord earnestly, and the believers who attended the conference were eager for the truth. During the five day New Spring Conference, believers brought cotton-wadded quilts and stayed overnight in the church. God's wonderful work was done through the ministers and believers there.

All the brothers and sisters who attended the Conference would willingly rise early and pray. The first day they got up to pray at five o'clock, the second day at four, and the last day about two in the morning! One could see their eagerness for God's truth.

One of the women came dressed in clothes customarily worn by the dead. She had almost died of an illness, and people had prepared burial clothes for her. However, God's great mercy came upon her and He delivered her from disease. She was in high spirits, "I wear such clothes because my illness brought me to the gate of death. I did not expect God to heal me, but now I not only live but can also walk twenty miles to attend the conference. It is by the wonderful power of God." When she spoke, her face was beaming. Later, she bought some steamed, filled buns to treat us and share her indescribable joy.

Seeing the believers seeking the truth during this conference, my heart was filled with thanks and praise. However, Satan became anxious and stirred up a minister in the nearby village to fight against us. Why? Because he was afraid that believers in his church would leave and join ours. Actually, there was no need for him to worry. The Lord Jesus is the head of the church and believers are parts of His body. Only the Lord has the supremacy to decide the function of every part. Besides, the brother in charge of this church would not be so selfish as to retain members of other churches for long.

Was it not good to feed believers spiritually through the conference? Yet that minister from the nearby church did not see the value but expressed his sinful nature. However, it is useless to obstruct the work of God.

Just before the conference, he addressed the brother in charge of the conference in an arrogant tone, which was not helpful for building up believers. Thus, the morning gathering was disturbed. I continued to put my hope in the Lord silently.

The angry minister sat in the first row, ready to create confusion. That day my message was on the second coming of Jesus with an object lesson. Believers should keep watch to meet the Lord. After my message, I gave the brothers and sisters a chance to confess. The minister who intended to harass the meeting was the first to confess his sin. This filled my heart with praises. The angels who watched his humble behavior surely must have rejoiced for his sincere repentance. Glory be to the triune God.

By the power of the Holy Spirit, we put to death the "self" and willingly let Jesus be our master, seeking His guidance in everything, eager to know His direction and revelation, and striving purposely to obey His will so that in everything He might have supremacy.

Chapter 4

The Way of the Cross

Following him fully

After China's civil war, there appeared articles tainted with flattery in some publications, among which there was one prayer written by elder Pastor Chen Chonggui, the President of *Chongqin Seminary*. Later I received a notice from the Christian YMCA asking me to register with the *Three-Self* organization, which was said to be led by the YMCA, and to attend their meetings. I went to the Lord to seek His guidance. He revealed to me His will, "Do not follow them."

The *Three-Self Protestant Patriotic Movement* in China stood for self-supporting, self-propagating, and self-governing. In the beginning, the leaders of the *Three-Self* organization promised not to interfere in the internal life of the churches as long as the churches did not receive money and administration from abroad. Later the organization gradually put the pressure on the ministry of the Lord through compulsory political study. By the winter of 1958, almost all the churches in the country, except for a few which were used as showcases to preach politicized sermons, were closed and church buildings were taken over for use as factories, shops, schools, warehouses, etc.

In 1953, Rev. Yang, pastor of *Wulumuqi Road Church*, invited me to take full charge of Children's Ministry in his church. To avoid jealousy which might cause unnecessary trouble, I declined his invitation. Again I sought God's will and was enlightened that I should be a maiden like Ruth to pick up leftover grain. To have more freedom to serve the Lord, I invited elder sister Shi to be the chairperson of the Gospel Center, while I myself preached there once a month as a volunteer.

On other Sunday mornings when I did not preach at the Center, I was invited to different churches to train Sunday School teachers and teach children. To avoid suspicions about my income, I became a piano teacher. I was classified as self-employed at the police station, and that was recorded in my residence booklet.

At first I did not understand what that designation meant. Later I learned that it indicated a group of self-employed professionals who belonged to no organization. I was responsible for my own living expenses and had no labor insurance. Those who worked in State-owned units received a pension when they reached retirement age.

When I began to teach piano, some people in the church thought that I had abandoned the gospel ministry and turned to the world. They did not realize that if I did not pursue the profession of a piano teacher, the police could send me to a labor camp at any time by accusing me of accepting money from churches abroad. Then some people offered to introduce me to work in the Literary and Art

Philharmonic Orchestra where a piano accompanist was needed. To reserve more time for the ministry of the Lord, I declined the offer, which made people suspicious that I did not want to serve non-Christians.

Some people kindly urged me to take a job in a State-owned organization, saying that churches would eventually be eliminated, with perhaps only one church remaining in the city. I did not listen to them. Day by day I followed my Lord with a simple heart. The Lord who searched my heart knew why I wanted to be self-employed. It was enough for me that the Lord knew whether I did it for temporal benefit or in observance of His will.

In the winter of 1955, a series of political accusation meetings were held in churches. It was announced that ministers had to join the *Three-Self,* an organization in essence controlled by atheists, whose officials would further control the pastors and ministers, and later also earnest Christians, of all churches. To please the *Three-Self* officials, some ministers made up stories or exaggerated facts against God's faithful servants who refused to join. As a result, several of them were arrested and imprisoned in the Anti-Revolutionary Campaign which spread all over the country bringing with it intense fear and terror. *Three-Self* officials spread terrible news in churches, urging ministers to join them.

One morning, an elder sister came from an indoctrination meeting and told me that ministers would have no future unless they attended political study. Then the Holy Spirit worked in my heart and told me: "The One who is in you is greater than the one who is in the world." I was so weak then that I prayed for help not to follow my flesh to pursue fame and gain like secular people, thus losing the presence and guidance of God.

At first, the pastor of the Gospel Center asked me to attend a study group for ministers in order to reform our ideology. Then the second daughter of Rev. Dai came to repeat the demand. She had been studying in *Xiangshan Grace Seminary*, Beijing, until the seminary was disbanded and authorities arrested. I began to examine circumstances like the situation that the apostle Peter found himself in. Seeing the wind and waves, my faith wavered, and I joined the political study as most people did.

One day we were studying the political slogan proposed by the government, "China would catch up with Great Britain within fifteen years and with the United States in twenty years." All people in the study group had to echo this nonsense. My heart was restless as I sat among that group of ministers, so I seldom spoke. Inwardly, I waited before God for guidance.

I thought that as a piano teacher it was not necessary to attend all those meetings. So when the district leader held a political accusation meeting against a minister-at-large, I left the assembly hall before the meeting finished, arousing suspicion that I was in sympathy with the minister being accused.

In 1957, officials from the *Religious Affairs Bureau* told the ministers and representatives of believers who attended the political study to "speak out freely and air views fully," namely to pour out all complaints and grievances against the Party and the government. Believing in their sincerity, a woman minister aired some complaints. She criticized a Western minister working in Ningbo, with whom she was familiar.

Unexpectedly, the woman minister was also to become a victim of a political accusation meeting. Now it was her turn to be criticized. A preparatory meeting was held for criticizing her. Officials from the *Religious Affairs Bureau* told me that I must attend. Everyone spoke something, and I was the last to speak. I said that I had known her for years and had never noticed her playing any political role. My speech incurred further pressure from the director of the study committee, a former pastor. He thought that I must be her good friend and urged me to denounce her relentlessly.

When the political accusation meeting began, many believers in her church denounced her. They mentioned her casual conversations, saying that she asked people to offer money to celebrate her husband's birthday and that she craved material things. Such meetings were held time and again.

Everyone was compelled to speak something. Under such circumstances, I was forced to say something against my own will. I said that she had mentioned in our study group that the Russian leaders did not pay homage to our country when they came to China and visited Hangzhou.

In the last political accusation meeting, I mentioned her complaint about the poverty of peasants. Then I asked her: "What stand did you take in saying that?" Immediately a voice in my heart asked: "What stand are *you* taking now?" I realized that I was pleasing man, thus sinning against the Lord. I prayed that the Lord would blot out my transgressions. From then on, I no longer attended the accusation meetings against that minister.

At the beginning of 1958, all ministers-at-large (not belonging to any churches) were incriminated as "anti-government." Rev. Wang, Pastor of the *Bread of Life Church* in Hongkou District, criticized me in our study group, saying that he should not have invited me to preach in his church. A few days later, the head of the study group drove me out of the study room, together with several other ministers who did not take formal jobs in churches, which made me very angry.

When I returned home and read God's Word, God spoke to me through Proverbs 12:16: "A fool shows his annoyance at once, but a prudent man overlooks an insult." God's Word calmed the billowing rage in my heart. Was my heart really calmed? No, waves would surge again within me when Satan trapped me by some casual rumor.

In the winter of 1957 my health was getting very poor, so I went to the district hospital for an examination. The medical reports showed that I suffered from cardiac hypertrophy. Later, I went to Chabei Hospital for new glasses. The optometrist, noticing my delicate health, suggested a rest in the countryside. At that time, the government urged people to settle in the countryside, so I thought he was speaking for the government, and took no notice of his suggestion.

Since I was very weak physically and tired all day long, I decided to take some Chinese medicine. The doctor advised me to improve my diet, besides taking Chinese medicine. She took my pulse and told me that my body consumed more energy than I took in. So I declined the job as a Sunday School teacher in a church, but invitations came in succession from other churches. I could find no excuse to refuse.

Some churches wanted me to lead women's fellowships, some hoped that I would hold a special youth meeting, while others invited me to head a revival conference, children's revival, etc. However, threats from *Three-Self* followed those meetings and my faith faltered. Oh, I was then just like a little worm that could not be touched, and I would die if I was touched.

How foolish of me to forget that many of God's faithful servants had passed through the Valley of Baca and shed sweat and blood. How can I be sitting in a bridal sedan chair and be carried into Heaven with ease? No, I cannot be like that. I must follow my Commander with all my heart, the One who loved me so much that He died for me.

I had to refuse everything that did not come from Him. There are no valuable things in the world that can be obtained without pay. The various branches of knowledge of the world are gained with much time and energy. Similarly, spiritual blessings cannot be possessed unless one is willing to abandon his or her life to gain a new life. The Bible says, "We have to pass through many tribulations before we enter the Kingdom of God." That is absolutely true.

The Lord saw that I hung my head like a bruised reed and was depressed in my spirit. He used an elderly lady to encourage and comfort me. All her sons, daughters and sons-in-law had very good jobs and she lived an affluent life, nevertheless Satan worked in her mind to want her to commit suicide. She even went out into the middle of the street, hoping to be run over by a car. She was sick and had poor eyesight, so she thought that it was better to be dead than alive.

Satan did not stop working in her until she met a doctor who persuaded her to trust in Jesus Christ. Someone introduced her to our Gospel Center. God's grace came upon her and she happily accepted the Lord Jesus Christ as her Savior. Since then her eagerness for the truth began to surpass that of average believers. The idea of committing suicide vanished. She bought a Bible with big characters and read it day and night. I was so encouraged by her changed life that I pulled myself up to again follow the Lord.

Concentrated indoctrination

In the spring of 1958 the political accusation meetings were held in churches again. To protect themselves, many ministers behaved the same way as secular people, and some were even more tricky and vicious. They were wheeling and dealing, fighting and striving, discriminating and detesting, with various kinds of furtive movements.

The evil things which filled the church turned God's temple into a den of robbers. Some pastors violated the Seventh Commandment and gave Satan a foothold to denounce them. Several believers from the Gospel Center also attended the political accusation meetings. The whole atmosphere was suffocating to the spiritual life of believers.

I felt that the Gospel Center was unable to survive under such circumstances, and the earlier it could be closed, the better. Sisters Shi and Huang had the same feeling. We both were quite certain that it was God's guidance, so we notified the regular attenders of the Center to go to worship service elsewhere. Everything in the Center was sold and the money from the sale was given to sister Shi and Huang, who were in charge of evangelism and visitation.

Sister Huang lived a simple life. She honored her father very much and was looking for a job to support him. Although there was no one concerned about her employment, God, who even took care of a little sparrow, did not forget this small maiden. A daughter of a believer from our Gospel Center wanted to set up a nursery school, so we transferred the two buildings of the Gospel Center to the Residents Committee for the nursery. When the Residents Committee opened a collectively State-owned school, they offered sister Huang a teaching position.

Although I did not accept any fee from preaching in the Gospel Center, God provided everything I needed. I did not post any leaflets on the street, nor did I tell anyone that I was recruiting piano students. But my God prepared proper students for me and led each of them to my house.

> Oh, the depth of the riches of the wisdom and knowledge of God! How unsearchable his judgments, and his paths beyond tracing out! Who has known the mind of the Lord? Or who has been his counselor? Who has ever given to God, that God should repay him? For from him and through him and to him are all things. To him be the glory forever! Amen (Romans 11:33-36).

After the closing of the Gospel Center, I heard that ministers were required to attend indoctrination classes. I prayed fervently that God would have mercy on me and save me from joining other ministers to attend such a study group. A few days later, the third daughter of Rev. Dai came to visit me, saying, "You must criticize from a political viewpoint the Sunday School materials that you compiled." It was impossible to criticize the materials that I wrote from a political view, which included stories of creation, the life of Jesus and parables taught by Jesus. Thank God, for He heard my crying and knew my weakness, because no more people came to ask me to criticize them.

Bad news came from those indoctrination classes. The brother in charge of the branch of *Shouzhen Church* committed suicide under the pressure of the group study. I was quite familiar with that brother and knew that he loved the Lord earnestly.

He worked hard to guide the believers in his branch into truth and there was a strong spiritual atmosphere in every gathering there, a sharp contrast to the lifeless services in the main church. It was very clear that he was a God-fearing man because every Tuesday he invited other ministers to come and help the believers. I was invited to hold gatherings in his branch for two months. Every time, the attendants would pack the sanctuary to its full capacity. However, wherever God works, there Satan will try hard to create disturbance.

That brother lived in the same house with the director of the main church. Perhaps, the director of the main church overheard some of his casual conversations, took them out of context and exaggerated them to please the officials from the *Three-Self* and *Religious Affairs Bureau*. The brother collapsed under the pressure and unfortunately went astray. How could I not feel grief and pity for him? As for me, this should have reminded me to retreat and wait for God's guidance. But I continued to teach piano.

In the early autumn of 1958, just when my eldest sister was looking for someone to accompany an old friend to Guangzhou, the eldest boy from our orphanage came from Shandong and promised to do that favor for my sister. I took the same train with them to Hangzhou to visit my elderly father.

My father lived in a building located in a very beautiful scenic spot. The house was surrounded by many artificial rocks and used to be a private villa. Now it was a permanent residence for several tenants. Looking at the tranquil surrounding, I was thinking of moving to Hangzhou to live with my father. I strolled up to the peak of the mountain and prayed. Then I recalled the story of Dr. R. A. Torrey when he climbed up the mountain with his fellow workers and prayed. How close they were to the Lord. And I felt contented before the Lord, too. I thought that it would be very nice to be able to read the Bible and pray in that quiet place. Suddenly, I was moved inwardly as I seemed to receive the message: "Three years." Without pondering the meaning of that message, nor seeking God's guidance, I hurried back to the train station.

At the train station I did not find the boy who accompanied my sister's friend to Guangzhou. However, he came to see me after I returned home. He told me that he still remembered life in the orphanage, the happiest time in his life. Thanks to our loving God, every student in the orphanage was plump and robust. Even the neighbors said that the students were blessed.

Later the sister-in-law of the student wrote to me, saying, "Our brother lost his mother when he was three months old and his father six years later. However, God provided him with a auntie like you, who treated him better than his parents. He is very lucky. If it were not for your raising our brother, he would have been deprived of education and would have lived in misery. Besides, your work helped him to grow spiritually, which will certainly please the Lord. Every time we talk about the orphanage, he looks very contented and happy, which shows the happiness in his heart. Many other orphans are equally blessed."

Several days later, I received a letter from another student of the orphanage. She graduated from *Anhui Medical College* and was a doctor now. She also remembered her happy childhood in the orphanage and expressed her gratitude. Unfortunately, the letter was taken away by the *Public Security Bureau* when my house was ransacked, and I lost contact with her.

Winter came without notice. Because I did not belong to any organization, the *Three-Self* asked the local police to arrange for my political study and to keep me under control. All ministers, except for a few used for political propaganda in churches, were forced to enter factories as workers. Church buildings were used as factories, canteens or other government facilities, and pianos from the sanctuaries were sold.

In October the local police station notified me to attend an indoctrination class in the neighborhood along with evildoers, thieves, robbers, and persons who were politically unreliable. The study lasted for ten days. At the last meeting, I was ordered to stand up among the group and was condemned by the director of the local police station. He criticized me for not earning my living through the Party. When I received this abuse by the director, my heart was filled with indescribable joy.

On my way home, I felt as if I was at the gate of the Kingdom of Heaven. Later, a policeman in charge of residents registration sent a child to tell me, "Go to register for a job." I thought that my job was teaching piano. Why should I register for another job? So I did not go, and nobody came to bother me again.

Then Satan took a chance to attack me and filled my heart with apprehension. I was harassed by weariness until God revealed to me in my prayer, "For in Him we live and move and have our being." The Lord says, "Your prayers and gifts to the poor have come up as memorial offerings before God." Having God's Word and His guidance, I enjoyed a thorough rest in the Lord with heavenly peace in my heart.

From all these things, God made it clear that His faithful ones shall carry their crosses to follow Him. Those who sincerely trust and obey God seem to suffer loss. However, they are blessed spiritually, because they can be closer to God with less sin and various blessings that many people have never dreamed of. Isaiah 48:21 says: "They did not thirst when the Lord led them through the deserts; he made water flow for them from the rock; he split the rock and water gushed out."

Faithful unto death

Here I relate an incredible story about a young brother named Miao Deqi. After graduating from the university, he was sent by the Party to teach in Shanxi. Because he read the Bible and prayed in his dormitory, the authorities of his school asked him to criticize his religion, which he refused. As a result, he was labeled as a hidden Rightist, and consequently was dismissed from the school.

Brother Miao was very simple and sincere. He would buy a birthday cake on his birthday and send it to my home. Although we only knew each other for a short time, we enjoyed each other's fellowship and our mutual concerns. His girl friend was also a devout Christian. She did not break her relationship with him because of his dismissal from school but encouraged him much.

After staying at home for a few months, he was sent, together with many bad elements and thieves, to Jiuquan, Gansu, to work in a wasteland. Among them was a pedicab driver from the Teachers College, where his father worked as a foreign language professor.

Brother Miao was very considerate and loved others earnestly. When he was going to leave, he firmly refused to accept the food ration from a relative who was working for the Lord. It was hard for a person like him to survive among a gang of hooligans who were used to stealing and extorting.

During that time, food was scarce in the country. Brother Miao could not get enough to each to sustain his heavy labor there. When his family sent some food to him from Shanghai, the people who were in charge of dispatching mail from the post office would consume the food. Some people could not stand the bitter life there and ran away. Brother Miao did not escape. He traded some of his clothes for food, but it did not help. At last, he could not bear the hunger and went with the pedicab driver to his brother's working unit in Lanzhou. His brother, seeing him badly sick, took him to the clinic, but the doctor there was a very selfish man. To draw a line between brother Miao and himself, he even said that Miao was pretending to be sick. He offered no treatment, no food, not even a tablet of medicine. Consequently, this precious brother in Christ died of starvation in Lanzhou.

Under such inhuman oppression, brother Miao sacrificed his life for the Lord. His life was like at white and fragrant rose, which was carried away by his Lord and planted in the glorious paradise. He would no longer suffer from fierce storms and scorching sun, hunger and thirst, or bullying by inhuman villains. The Lamb on the throne will take care of him and lead him to the spring of living water where he will enjoy everlasting rest. Brother Miao, a dear son of God, is waiting for the glorious day of resurrection with numerous soldiers of Christ who sacrificed their lives for the Lord.

Having heard the news of his death, brother Miao's girl friend fell into indescribable grief. However, the Lord Jesus, who had worn the crown of thorns, understood her bitterness and sheltered her under His pierced side to comfort her. Like healing ointment, the Holy Spirit was able to heal her wound and strengthen her faith, which enabled her to love God and her neighbors with His unquenchable love.

She lost her mother in childhood and was brought up by her father. Later she came down with tuberculosis, resulting in the removal of several ribs. She certainly didn't expect her fiance to die before their wedding. However, she uttered no complaint nor lost hope. She lifted up her tearful eyes to Christ, her Lord, and ran with perseverance the race marked out for her.

With such unbearable misery in her heart, she managed in her busy schedule to visit a lonely and weak sister who lost her companion and was despised, deserted and humiliated by her neighbors and colleagues in her school. By her concern for others, she manifested the amazing power of the Lord, proclaimed the marvelous triumph of Jesus and exalted the glory of God before angels, Satan and the world, the glory of the inheritance of the saints. In a grove of thorns, brother Miao's girl friend grew into a pure white lily, beautiful, bright, and fragrant.

A thread of light from dawn

The persecutions and deaths of sister Du Hengwei and brother Miao Deqi filled my heart with indescribable anguish. Should I sit still? No, I should live for the Lord as His dedicated maiden. Then, how should I serve the Lord? I was at a loss and suffered from a heavy burden. So I went to the bookcase to look for a book to read in order to be strengthened from the example of another believer-pilgrim's progress.

When the missionaries of the *China Inland Mission* were forced to leave the country in 1951, they did not carry away all their books. Brother Wesley Milne let me have some from what they left. Later brother Li of *Endeavors Church* also gave me some books. Being very busy, I had only read a few of them so far.

As I was browsing, I noticed one book, *The Prayer Life* by Andrew Murray. Like a lamp shining in the darkness, the book gave light to pilgrims who did not know where to go and guided them onto the right path. Although I did not write smoothly, I thought I should translate that book into Chinese in my spare time so that my fellow workers in Christ could read it. At that time the ministers and believers in our country seemed to be wrapped in pitch-darkness as if before a great storm, when people could not discern even a thread of the light of truth through thick clouds.

My Heavenly Father moved a sister from the *Shanghai Seminary* to edit my translation. That sister graduated from a university in Hangzhou in 1951, then taught in a county school in Zhejiang. Later, God called her to serve Him full-time so she entered the seminary in Shanghai. She studied there until 1958. Even though she was weak physically, she and all other students in the seminary were assigned to work in factories after receiving socialist education.

Guided by the Holy Spirit, she left the factory by faith and began her ministry of personal evangelism. She forsook everything to preach the gospel. God provided her everything for her living. In her difficult circumstances, 2 Timothy 4:2 was always in her mind. "Preach the word; be prepared in season and out of season; correct, rebuke and encourage. . .with great patience and careful instruction." With strong faith and pure love for the Lord, this sister prepared oil along with her lamp like a wise virgin. In the light from her lamp, many fumbling in the darkness were able to get onto the bright heavenly path.

On the second day of Chinese New Year in 1961, brother Wang came to see me saying, "Mr. Jiang and a deacon from *Shouzhen Church* invite you to pray with us in my home tomorrow." I said that I had an appointment and could not go to his home, but brother Wang insisted that I should go. He said that Mr. Jiang had already visited him twice and needed someone to pray with him. In that case, I agreed to go. Recalling the brother in charge of the branch of the church who had committed suicide, I decided not to overlook Jiang's need for prayer.

The following day, I was waiting in brother Wang's home for Mr. Jiang and was ready to pray. I was surprised to see that Mr. Jiang was very nervous, looking around furtively as he entered the room, but I never dreamed that he had ulterior motives. When I saw him, I could not keep from crying.

Not until I was arrested and confined in the detention house did I realize that my tears forecasted the tribulations that I was to undergo. The Holy Spirit knew the troubles ahead and warned me with such tears. At noon that day I fasted and got a word from God:

> I keep asking that the God our Lord Jesus Christ, the glorious Father, may give you the Spirit of wisdom and revelation, so that you may know him better. I pray also that the eyes of your heart may be enlightened in order that you may know the hope to which he has called you, the riches of his glorious inheritance in the saints, and his incomparably great power for us who believe. (Ephesians 1:17-18)

In his prayer, Jiang said that he had experienced many tribulations. When we finished praying, I hurried back home without talking with Jiang because a boy from our orphanage was to have dinner with me that evening. It was God's protection. Because my time of distress had not come yet, so Satan could not harm me. Many times, God's hand of mercy already shades us before we know it. His light of grace is always brightening our journey in darkness. However, I did not understand God's arrangement and guidance then.

Chapter 5

Prison on the Horizon

A voice from heaven

Less than a month after I prayed with Jiang in brother Wang's home, he came to my home. He said that his labor in the factory was so heavy that he often got dizzy and had to refresh himself with cold water. His feet were swollen, but he was not allowed to take sick leave because he had no high fever. His wife had been labeled a Rightist for years with reduced pay. Quarrels broke out between them from time to time over financial problems. His children were despised and mocked at school. I listened with sympathy.

At each visit he would talk about the misery of his family. His children were hungry and took turns licking the rice soup pot. Sister Huang and I often invited him to have dinner with us. Sometimes, we would give him food coupons saved from our own rations.

In those days, people in the country were having a hard time. Food was scarce. A ten cent egg was sold for fifty cents, also the price of half a kilo of green vegetables. There were even times when one could not buy food. Sister Huang and I did our best to support him with food, thinking that he consumed more energy than we did, and that his children needed sufficient nourishment.

In the summer of 1961, Jiang talked with me about the political situation in the country. So I mentioned the names of the leaders of the country in my prayer, asking God not to allow Satan to work upon them. Sometimes, I would let Jiang read my translation of *The Prayer Life*. He said that he hoped to make a copy for his own use, but he needed some paper, which I readily gave him. In fact, he was lying to me. Pretending to be an angel of light, he deceived me into praying with him. Then he exaggerated what I said in my prayer which he reported to the government officials.

Several months passed. Noticing the stagnant growth of Jiang's spiritual life, I talked with a godly sister about him. That sister said, "It is no wonder that his spiritual life does not grow in such circumstances, in which we ourselves might not make any progress spiritually. Besides, he has a family to support, and his labor leaves him little time for personal devotions." I agreed with her, so continued to pray with him. Sometimes I lent him some Christian literature.

One day, as I was closing the door before prayer, I sensed an inner warning, "What about the man *inside* the door?" With the door closed behind me, I was puzzled, but still prayed with him. Actually, I should have followed more closely the guidance of the Holy Spirit. Unfortunately, I

chose to follow my own path instead of God's, thus unconsciously occupying the place which belonged to God. How
I sinned against Him by doing so!

One day when Jiang had lunch at our home, I asked
him to read a few pages of my translation after lunch. While
he was reading, I went to the restroom. As soon as I reached
the door of the restroom, I heard a voice warning me:
"Prison and hardships are facing you." I was stunned.
Then, all was dead silence. I stood for a while, then returned
to the living room. He said, "I have finished the reading." I
knew that he was lying. It was impossible to finish within
such a short time. Still I made excuses for him, thinking that
he was obliged to say so due to some urgent errand.

Although I was so foolish, my patient, merciful Lord
kept on warning me. It was near the end of the year. An
elderly believer, our former cook who lived nearby, came to
sell me some soybeans. Since Jiang was in the living room,
I took her into sister Huang's room because I was afraid that
she would tell the policeman about him. I bought a kilo of
soybeans from her and returned to the door of the living
room, when I heard again a clear voice of warning from
heaven, "The person outdoors is good, and the one *indoors*, bad," which later proved to be true.

One day, the policeman in charge of residents registration asked that elder believer what I had said to her. She
answered, "Nothing meaningful." He continued, "Has she
prayed with anyone?" She shook her head. When she was
asked if any old man came to my home, she gave a firm "no"
again and blamed the policeman for suspecting me.

Later, the policeman came to my house to check my
Bible. Another time, when a godly sister was in my house,
the policeman came to examine her handbag but found
nothing. When those unusual things happened, I should
have been very cautious and sought God's guidance in

everything. However, I still busily engaged myself in trans-lation and writing. How foolish I was, but God did not stop working on me. He guided me step-by-step to know His power and will.

In the winter of 1961, I bought two egg-laying hens at a high price to improve our meager diet. I set a hen house on the balcony of the second floor. Sister Huang cleaned the coop every day. Besides outer leaves of vegetable, I often bought some worms for the hens. Thus, we could collect one or two eggs a day.

One day when I opened a window on the balcony, one of the hens suddenly jumped out. It flew all the way down, landing on the street. I was surprised indeed. The hens used to walk on the balcony peacefully. Why did one of them dash out like a spark of fire? Although I was very confused, I was directed by God to find the hen.

The poor little thing hid in a dark and damp corner under a vegetable vendor's stand, which blocked the way on both sides of our house. Watching the hen from the window above, I called sister Huang to go to the street, pull it out of that dark corner and bring it back. Sister Huang blamed me for not going downstairs with her to catch the hen. I told her, "I have to watch, lest it be carried away by some passerby. Besides, since I am watching, you will know where to find it." She was no longer annoyed with me.

I was timid by nature. Through that little incident, God taught me the truth, which I never forgot whether in hardship or misery, that I was bought by the blood of the Lord. I totally belong to Him. God made me and will never forget me. He was, is and will be Almighty God forever. His sovereignty is over all. The enemy cannot go beyond the boundary set by the Lord. He moves quietly and assuredly until His own are led to a secure place.

One day, when Jiang talked with me about brother

Wang, I asked him to tell Wang, "The year is drawing to an end. Pray hard before God, and pray at home with brothers and sisters nearby, because it is improper for a young man to stay idle at home." I also told him that sister Huang, two other sisters and I would pray overnight at New Year's Eve.

A few days later, Jiang came to say that brother Wang and he would come to pray with me on New Year's Eve, which I thought was inappropriate. So I went to ask elderly Mrs. Qiu if she had any plans for New Year's Eve, hoping that they could join Qiu's prayer group. She said, "No!" Her granddaughter added that Jiang was poor spiritually.

When I returned home, I especially prayed for that event. God let me see His Word in Acts 2:1: "All with one accord in one place." I neglected the words "with one accord" and only noticed "in one place," so I let them come to our prayer meeting.

During that meeting, I remembered the martyrdom of sister Du Hengwei, her mother and sisters, and prayed for them. In my prayer, I quoted the verse: "The grass withers and the flowers fall" (Isaiah 40:7). I never dreamed that Jiang would report it to the government as part of the evidence to incriminate me.

On New Year's morning, brother Wang came to borrow six pictures to be used for preaching. Noticing that he was followed by the policeman in charge of residents registration, I asked him to buy the pictures from a Christian bookstore. When he saw the policeman behind him, brother Wang stopped visiting me. Jiang volunteered to take my translation to brother Wang and bring me back the clean copy, which I considered an earnest service from a willing heart. I was a real fool.

One evening Jiang came to tell me that he still wanted to preach the gospel and asked me to pray for him. The day before Spring Festival, I invited Jiang and brother

Wang to come over for lunch. We spent time singing and praying.

On the third day of the festival, I went out in the evening to give piano lessons to three students who lived on Yongan Lane. Since one of the students asked for sick leave, I took the chance to go to brother Wang's home to see sister Ying. Brother Wang had invited a fellow believer from his church, brother Bao, to have dinner. Jiang was accompanying them.

Brother Bao, whose parents were nonbelievers, was the only son in his family. After he graduated from the Architecture Department of *Tongji University*, he was imprisoned for several years for refusing to attend the political indoctrination classes organized by the *Three-Self*. When he completed his sentence, he was assigned to work as a laborer in Qinghai, Northwest of China.

He returned to Shanghai now to settle the divorce case appealed to the court by his wife. Though a Christian, she fell in love with another young Christian, her co-worker in the hospital, and decided to divorce brother Bao. It proved the Word in 2 Timothy 3:3: "People will be ... brutal, not lovers of good, treacherous, rash. . . ."

After dinner, brother Wang led us in a song in remembrance of sister Du Hengwei. Then we all knelt to pray. My prayer was as follows: "Vindicate your children Lord, have revenge and deliver us, God. Bring back the captive, open the eye of the blind and give freedom to the oppressed. . . ." Nobody thought that Jiang reported my prayer as evidence for my imprisonment. It proved the Word of the Lord Jesus: "A man's enemy will be members of his own household" (Matthew 10:36).

To comfort brother Bao's wounded heart, I invited him to have dinner in my home two days later, together with Jiang, brother Wang and two sisters in Christ. After dinner, we specifically prayed that the Lord would show him His favor and strengthen him.

On the following day, something unexpected happened to brother Bao and he was forced to return to Xining. When I met Jiang, I asked if he mentioned brother Bao to anyone. He stared at me for a while and answered, "No." Actually, he was dead to all feelings. Indulging in sin and doing shameful things, he had already deteriorated to such an extent as to lose any sense of reproach.

A miraculous thing happened to me on a Wednesday afternoon in June 1962. When I was walking from my bedroom to the bathroom after finishing my fasting prayer, I suddenly heard a voice from heaven clearer than before saying, "Everything you have done is known to the local police station." I asked, "Who told them?" The answer was, "Jiang." Having heard the voice, I should have prepared myself to face the consequences. However, I was just too foolish to be ready for it. (I remind the reader not to pursue after visions or voices. It will give Satan a foothold if one indulges in seeking such voices.)

God's plan would not be changed because of my foolishness. As it is written in Proverbs 16:4: "The Lord works out everything for His own ends—even the wicked for a day of disaster." What happened to me a few days later proved the solemn warning from God.

A blind servant, deaf messenger was I, who did not understand her master's guidance and acted according to her own ideas. However, God's full knowledge will be revealed and His prophecy fulfilled in due time. His thoughts are not our thoughts, neither are our ways His ways. The fact that I was warned again and again before the trouble came helped me to survive the prison life and false accusations. Still, like the hen in the arms of sister Huang, I can happily rest in the arms of my Sovereign, Almighty God of love, who is absolutely holy and faithful, omnipotent and omniscient.

Go out!

To face the uncertain future for both believers and the church, we felt it necessary to hold a prayer meeting at the end of 1961. It was held overnight, so that everyone could concentrate his or her mind on prayer without being interrupted.

That night, sister Li prepared a box holding several hundred pieces of Bible promises. After prayer, each of us drew a promise from the box. The verse I drew was Isaiah 52:12: "You will not leave in haste or go in flight; for the Lord will go before you, the God of Israel will be your rear guard." That verse has stayed vivid in my heart ever since.

On New Year's morning, after saying grace for breakfast, we each first drew a number and then found our seat according to the number. On every seat there was a verse of promise. What a surprise that on my seat I found Isaiah 52:12 again! It was even a wonder that an unfamiliar sister from Tianjin wrote to me, using the same verse in her letter. She also added Esther 4:14: "Who knows but that you have come to a royal position for such a time as this?"

When I happened to pick up a newspaper, the verse in an article which caught my eye was again Isaiah 52:12. To receive the same verse four times made me think that God would lead me out. In that period of time, I often ran across the word "go out" in my morning and evening Bible reading.

It happened that sister Hsu Liu Yutang wrote to invite me to take a break in her home. So I thought that I would be going to Hong Kong. Actually, that was not in God's plan. What God wanted to tell me with that verse was that He would lead me out of my home and take care of me.

Apart from that verse, God also gave me a verse from Acts 15:16: "After this I will return and rebuild David's fallen tent. Its ruins I will rebuild and I will restore it."

On Easter Eve 1962, we held another overnight prayer meeting. Our purpose was to thank God for the completion of the translation and to see His guidance for each of our futures and for a booklet I wrote titled, *Rise and Pray.* The contents included the following messages: 1) to whom shall we pray, 2) who can pray, 3) how to pray, 4) when to pray, 5) for what shall we pray, 6) the barriers to prayer, and 7) examples of prayer being heard. In the picture which would be used as the cover of the booklet was of a man lying in bed, reluctant to get up, a clock on the wall pointing to a late hour in the morning and a cock crowing. The picture was to remind every believer not to give themselves up to deep sleep, but to get up promptly and pray.

I had hoped to take the manuscript to Hong Kong and have it published. In May, I went to the local police station to apply for going to Hong Kong. On my way back home, I got a word from God, Luke 1:49: "For the mighty one has done great things for me." I thought that meant I would be able to leave for Hong Kong, but I did not know that God's will was better than that. He had a greater mission for me—to bear witness for Him before His enemy. All these I did not understand until later. Then I realized how great and awesome were those things God had done for me.

Mrs. Chiu, Pastor Stephen Chiu's wife and my co-worker in the orphanage, wrote to me, saying that she had prepared housing for me in Hong Kong. Another sister in Christ, Mrs. Yu Yuren, missed me too. Sister Yu stayed in Shanghai for years. Her husband wanted to divorce her and she was very depressed. We prayed for her and I often wrote her letters. God heard our prayers and the couple was reconciled. Her husband bought a house for her in Hong Kong, so she moved there. When she learned of the situation in the country, she sent me some food to Shanghai. The concern of sisters in Christ from whom I had been separated for years reminded me of the great love of God, which I could not express fully with my tongue or describe well with my pen.

During our last overnight prayer meeting, God comforted me with His word: "The Lord is righteous in Him. He never does anything unrighteous. Every morning, the Lord will show His righteousness. *He fails not.*" I had read the Bible for years, but never noticed these words. However, before the tribulation, the Lord showed me the message and made it particularly attractive to me. Can it be anyone else but the Lord Himself who strengthens my faith by the message? God never disappoints me, as long as it will do me good. He also will not fail me, if I love the Lord with all my heart and all my soul and all my mind.

A month later, I went to the local police station to ask about my application to go to Hong Kong. The policeman in charge of residents registration answered, "No." When I walked home, I got a word from God: "There is no path that you cannot find a way out at the end of it."

Arrested!

It was July 2, 1962, after seven in the evening. The director of our Residents Committee, the policeman in charge of residents registration and policemen from the Security Bureau swarmed into my living room. Satan, the head of the spiritual forces of evil in the heavenly realms, suddenly shone a beam of light before me, saying, "Go to Hong Kong!" The policemen locked my hands with iron cuffs, took out an official arrest warrant and ordered me to sign it.

They threw out all the books from my bookshelves and searched for my translation manuscript. Then they took away the manuscript of the booklet, *Rise and Pray*. In the meantime, sister Huang was crying in her room. I asked the director of our Residents Committee to send for her so that I could give her some money and a small clock. A policeman wanted to stop me. I said, "She has no watch." Then they let her have it.

I also left her some eggs and other food, something prepared for her by the Lord. Sister Huang had gone to Hangzhou for Spring Festival before Lunar New Year, and I gave all our food to Jiang. When she came back, she had nothing to eat. I had been saving the food for my visit to my father on July fourth. I never thought that I would be arrested before that day.

When leaving home, I saw sister Huang crying, so I said to her, "What are you crying for? I am willing to die for Jesus." Then I handed all the things to her, thinking I would die in the prison.

I asked for a small Bible, which was rejected by the policeman, so I said to sister Huang, "Let us pray for each other." Thus, we parted. In people's eyes, the happening seemed to be a terrible loss. However, the Lord was still my refuge.

About 9:30 that evening, I was taken to the *Public Security Bureau*, Hongkou Branch. On arrival, I was finger printed, searched, and taken to a small cell where I had to sleep on the floor. The youngsters also detained in that room were pickpockets, thieves, prostitutes and profiteers. I took the chance to preach the gospel and teach them to sing hymns. Two or three days later, the director of the detention house warned me that I was not allowed to preach the gospel. However, I could still serve the Lord and praise Him through prayer. He did take care of me according to His faithfulness.

One night, in the midst of my dreams, a profiteer woke me up and gave me some delicious refreshment she had brought into the house. Who could imagine that I would have such good food from a stranger in that miserable place. Praise the Lord, O my soul!

A few days later, the interrogator sent for me. I was ordered to sit on a very low stool. Being a criminal I should be lower than average people! The interrogator asked me, "Who copied the book?" I answered, "It is copied by the copier." Then she asked again, "Who read the book?" I said, "Read by the reader." This interrogation lasted for more than two months.

The *Security Bureau* notified my elder sister, asking her to persuade me to be cooperative. My elder sister wrote letters to me saying that she was to be blamed because she did not render me enough help. I was sad to read her letters, thinking that I dragged her into trouble for something that had nothing to do with her.

By late September, a section chief in the detention house asked if I would let my eldest sister take home my watch, keys and receipts. I said yes, so he gave them to her and she brought me things that I needed. Then I asked her to break the rental contract of my housing so that she would not have to pay rent for me any longer, but the interrogator told her to keep it for me, in case of future usage. He also said that it was slow suicide to refuse to confess, however, he and a section chief in the detention house were rather kind to me.

In the height of the summer, there were so many women in the detention house that several dozen people had to be packed into a small cell with only a tiny hole for ventilation. The atmosphere in the room was so suffocating that I could hardly breathe. My heart condition worsened and I thought I would die. Then God directed me to dampen a small piece of towel in the water running into the toilet, and put it on my forehead and nostrils. I was much refreshed.

God told me "Go through Samaria." Instantly I pictured the Lord Jesus sitting by the well of Samaria, tired, thirsty, hungry and sleepy (see John 4:6). I had to go through Samaria "to fill up in my flesh what is still lacking in regard to Christ's affliction" (Colossians 1:24). Was it not an honor?

Besides the suffocating heat, I was infected with lice, brought by several young women arrested from train stations or boats. We were packed like canned sardines and lice spread to everyone. Fortunately, sister Hsu Liu Yutang sent me a light color silk blouse and nylon sweater, which I could use as undergarments and which were easy to wash. Small and short, the nylon sweater was warm wrapped on my body. Through the nylon, I could see the lice clearly and catch them easily. That nylon sweater was with me for seventeen winters in prison and labor camp. I keep it as a souvenir.

By God's mercy the officials asked my eldest sister to visit me. She came to see me once a month. Usually, such visits were forbidden, but my eldest sister was an exception. To assist the officials of the Security Bureau, she came to persuade me to write down my story.

The interrogator promised that nobody would be persecuted and that I would be released as long as I confessed. Because Jiang had known everything and had sent the translation manuscript to brother Wang, I answered one by one the questions about the translation of the book, prayer meetings, etc. I wrote my confession in the director's office.

In the room next to the office there was a young man locked in alone. When there was nobody in the office, he called in a low voice, "Bible, Bible." I dared not answer him. I was afraid to be heard by other people and get into trouble. It seemed that he was desperately in need of a Bible. It was a pity that I could not help him. I could only pray for him silently.

Later the interrogator asked again about the pamphlets compiled by brother Wang. However, I would not tell them anything about other people, not even if I would have to stay in prison two years longer for it. Besides, I had not read the pamphlets, so was ignorant of their contents. I was determined not to sin against God for my own benefit, so I kept silent.

One day, I saw some workers in the detention house making mops outside our cell. They gave a hard pull to each strip. If a strip did not break under the pull, it would be left; otherwise, it would be thrown away. This showed me that those used by God shall go through trials. If you persevere with a willing heart, the Lord accepts you, and it is vitally important to stand firm under trial.

In the detention house I met all sorts of people. A woman was arrested for trading rice coupons. One day when someone wanted to buy coupons from her, she was arrested. Another woman was struck by swine epilepsy one night and laid on the ground like a dead person. She made no end of pig-like squealing and people shrank from her with fear. I was the only one who would sit beside her, and I quietly prayed for her. The director and the chief saw what I did, which hopefully impressed them.

Satan not only worked on others but also on me. I suffered from serious heart trouble, which caused muscle spasms all over my body. Lice multiplied on my head and body. My eldest sister bought me a double-edged, fine-toothed comb which I used every day, and eventually got rid of the lice on my head. She also took my clothes to wash and boil, and the lice on my body decreased.

Because I was in very poor health, the director allowed my sister to send me boiled eggs as well as medicine twice a month, which were prohibited according to the regulations. The regular meals were two bowls of rice soup and one bowl of steamed rice a day, with salted vegetable, pickles and dried radish mixed with some dried sweet potatoes. Occasionally, we would have hollow-stem greens and pumpkin.

Some young inmates were very nimble. A soon as the meal containers appeared at the small window on the door, they would snatch the containers and pour part of the rice soup or rice from my container into theirs. I did not argue over such a trifle, because they did need more food.

In the midsummer, it was stifling in the crowded cell and the air was foul and stinking. The function of my heart became so abnormal that you could hear a sound like running water from my heart. The director locked my hands and sent me to the prison hospital for medical treatment. A senior doctor examined me and said that I had rheumatoid arthritis for years.

Satan not only attacked me bodily, he also attacked me spiritually. I was timid and discouraged. For a long time, I did not read the Bible, and I could not concentrate in prayer with so many people crowded in the small and noisy cell; I was very weak spiritually, unable to seize God and wrestle with Him like Jacob at the ford of Jabbok. Satan continued to disturb my mind, saying: "The mighty one has done great things for you. Where are those great things now?"

I hated my foolishness in not taking notice of God's warning. I reproached myself for not leaving Shanghai earlier like my smart fellow workers. When I was blaming myself, God's word came upon me: "It does not depend on man's desire or effort, but on God's mercy" (Romans 9:16). Still I hated myself bitterly.

I thought that there were many people like Jiang in the church and I hoped that I could get out of prison early to warn others that they should guard against false brothers and sisters. If I had been betrayed by a nonbeliever, I would not feel so hurt. But being sold out by the senior pastor of a church, resulting in damage to my ministry and the loss of the manuscripts of my translation, I felt such bitterness as I had never tasted before.

In the midst of such agony, the Lord comforted me. He reminded me that I had preferred to be a victim like Jesus than an evil one like Cain. In silence the Lord spoke to me in His soft voice: "I was also ranked with the criminals."

In the Christmas of 1962, brother Wang was also arrested and sent to the branch of *Security Bureau,* because he had compiled some small pamphlets. During Spring Festival of the following year, my eldest sister brought some tangerines to me. The director ordered me to eat them in his office. A guard asked the director why they did not set me free. The director said it was because I was "deeply poisoned," meaning I was so firm in my faith and would rather die for my faith than give in.

In fact, I was not that firm. After the admonishment of the director, I dared not do anything more than pray silently. I lost my strength to evangelize.

A second detention house

By March of 1963 I was sent with a batch of male prisoners to the Second Detention House on Masinan Road. I was so weak spiritually that I cried on my way there. Then I recalled that I had once blamed a minister who cried when she was imprisoned in Qinghai Labor Camp, as I believed that a Christian should not cry in the presence of nonbelievers. Now God let me see that I was not stronger than others because I could not help crying.

When I was climbing into the paddy wagon, the director bid me not to tell the people in the Second Detention House that I had heart disease. He was afraid that the officials there would refuse to accept me and return me back to him. And when the interrogator saw that I was short of breath, he went to open a little window, a three inch square opening on the top of the wagon. Except for the area under that window, there was pitch-darkness inside, just like the darkness before an earthquake, the darkness in which people lose any hope for the dawn.

When I arrived at the Second Detention House and was fingerprinted, the first order by the male guard was, "You cannot pray." I did not say anything, but I prayed hard inwardly. Then an idea struck me that I could still say grace with my eyes open before meals, and I did so.

That afternoon there was an indoctrination class. Several people said that I no longer prayed with my eyes closed. One woman said that she used to see me play the piano in the church. Immediately I was convicted by the Holy Spirit. I realized that my weakness came from my desire to please man. I had sinned against God, and lost my witness as a Christian before nonbelievers. From then on, I decided that by the power of the Holy Spirit I would say grace with my eyes closed no matter what the circumstances.

Every Sunday afternoon, prisoners were ordered to wash their heads. I saw others use water four times, so I did the same. One day when the director saw it, she scolded me for being dishonest. I answered, "I used water four times every time I wash my head, not only today." She was very angry, but could do nothing about it.

Since I had no physical activity in the detention house, my joints became very stiff, and they cracked whenever I moved. Even so, the director did not allow my relatives to send me cod liver oil pills. Sometimes, I had to force myself to swallow some half meal container of very bitter vegetables as nourishment.

The director regarded me, a believer in Christ, as a chief criminal. She even stopped my supply of toilet paper. It was very inconvenient because I was in the menopausal period and needed much toilet paper from time to time. Thanks to my gracious God, a female guard took pity and gave me a supply of toilet paper. That guard also felt that the verdict in my case was unjust. When I was almost suffocating at night, she would open the window for me.

One day, the director came with guards to examine my belongings. They threw my things all over the place. After they left, I could not find my winter cream. I looked everywhere for it but in vain. Then I thought that it might have been taken by my cell mate, because there were only two of us in the cell. She often took my things for her own use.

When I was tidying up my things, my cell mate asked what I was looking for. I said that my cream was missing. At that moment, a very rude guard came by. My cell mate rushed to her to report my story. Without asking me any questions, the guard immediately scolded me fiercely. It was the first time that I had been framed by such a wrongdoer. I shivered with fury; my heart was surging with rage.

In the detention house, each prisoner could have a cup of hot water every day, for drinking only. One day, I used that cup of water for some special need, and I was bitterly reproached again. God had His purpose to let me deal with such unreasonable guards, because I had not learned to die with the Lord yet and had not truly experienced the death of my old self. Otherwise, I would have rejoiced "also in our sufferings, because we know that suffering produces perseverance; perseverance, character; and character, hope, and hope does not disappoint us" as Paul teaches in Romans 5:3-6.

Unfortunately, I had not put my old self to death yet. So my heart would be stirred whenever the wind blew, and I would envy the wicked. I am ashamed of myself even now when I recall that experience. I should have received all these sufferings with joy to learn to die with the Lord.

Without experiencing the death of the old Adam nature, how could I bear witness for the Lord and how could I help those who also suffered from wrongdoers? The Lord knew that my heart was filled with wrong accusations, so He comforted me with the following verse from a famous poem: "I wonder no more passing ahead at the end of the path, when appears a village shadowed with willow and brightened with flower." God revealed to me that there would be a new and beautiful oasis after this seemingly endless desert of misery.

Why should I be disturbed by the foggy present and vague future? Since the Almighty, All-wise God is at the helm of my ship, I should be confident with hope and joyful with peace even though it seemed that the ship would be buried in the stormy sea. Everything would be all right as long as I surrendered myself to the Lord by faith. Praise the Lord, O my soul!

Chapter 6

A Criminal in Prison

Sentenced to ten years

The living conditions in the Second Detention House were much better than in the police station. Here prisoners took baths together in one big tub, for which I could do nothing but entrust myself to the Lord.

However, I suffered greater pressure spiritually in the Second Detention House. Never had I encountered such rude and arrogant persons as our female director and one of the guards. Now God allowed these wicked ones so that I, a servant of Jesus Christ, might experience physical and spiritual tortures, sympathize with those who were in suffering and demonstrate my faith in the Lord by the power of the Holy Spirit. Just as Job said, "Though He slay me, yet will I hope in him" (Job 13:15).

After several months in the Second Detention House,

a public prosecutor came to interrogate me. I told him that I was very sorry about the death of innocent Du Hengwei, who was even accused for being single, and I answered his questions with loud crying. So they locked me in a padded cell where people would not hear my crying.

Later, there came another interrogator. He was very gentle. I told him that the workers in the detention house were brutal; they regarded me, a believer in Jesus, as a thorn in the flesh and a nail in the eye. My joints were all swelling and very sore, but I was not allowed to receive cod-liver oil pills from my relatives. I also talked about the tragic death of Du Hengwei. Even her family knew nothing about her death. The interrogator asked, "How do you know that she is dead?" Then he tried hard to confuse me so that I would not be too grief-stricken. After that, the director and the guards treated me much better.

My last interrogation was handled by a young woman who was proud and conceited. She asked me if I had attended gatherings in other places besides Wang's. By the grace of the Lord, I bravely answered, "I was not under surveillance. Why couldn't I walk around? I am not satisfied with the death of Hengwei who died without being tried." She replied, "The more deaths there are of anti-revolutionaries, the better." I retorted vehemently, "Was she an anti-revolutionary? Show me the evidence of her being an anti-revolutionary." Thus ended the interrogation.

On November 20, 1963, I was sent in handcuffs to the Hongkou District Court, where I was sentenced to ten years imprisonment. The judge ordered me to sit down to listen to my verdict. Then he asked if I had any requests. I asked to see my elderly father, but my request was ignored.

Actually, the judge had no alternative in my case. Anyone who attended family church gatherings or distributed Christian literature was labeled anti-revolutionary, according to China's religious policy at that time. The following was my verdict:

> Public Prosecutor: Zhi-Kwen Ho, Prosecutor of Hongkou District People's Court, Shanghai.
> The Accused: Wang Chunyi, Female, 49 years old, native of Wujin, Jiangsu;
> Permanent address: 365 Ermei Road, Shanghai.
> Brief of the Case: Anti-revolutionary.
>
> By Public Prosecutor Zhi-Kwen Ho, Hongkou, Shanghai

The case has been heard and concluded by the above mentioned court. It is evident that the accused, Wang Chunyi, has been persistently hostile to the people's democratic regime. Covered with a cloak of religion, she actively carried out anti-revolutionary activities. From 1960, the accused has secretly translated and compiled reactionary literature, *Rise and Pray*, etc., and distributed the books as far as to Guangzhou, Zhejiang and other places to spread the poison of anti-revolutionary ideology and instigate believers to oppose the government.

The accused, together with anti-revolutionary, Wang Zhongxiao, often mustered some other believers to attend illegal "family church gatherings," which sometimes lasted throughout the night. During those gatherings, they wantonly vilified and defiled the policy and decree of the Party and government, cursed the Party's and country's leaders in their prayer, using the metaphor of "the grass withers and flowers fail" to express their vain hope of the downfall of the People's Regime and of the comeback of the anti-revolution.

In the meantime, the accused complained loudly about the grievance for an anti-revolutionary, who was executed by the government. In a witnessing gathering, held by the anti-revolutionary, Wang Zhongxiao, for an anti-revolutionary released from labor reform camp, Biao Weiyuan, the accused and Wang Zhongxiao actively promoted anti-revolutionary incitation.

The facts of the crime committed by the above mentioned accused are evidenced by the accusation and denunciation of the masses and by the seized anti-revolutionary literature compiled in handwriting by the accused, and proved true by the confession of the criminal of the same case.

The above mentioned court believes the accused, covered with a religious cloak, actively promotes anti-revolutionary propaganda and incitation in the vain hope to overthrow the rule of the People's Democratic Regime and state the comeback of anti-revolution, thus has committed a serious crime, which deserves punishment.

According to Issue 10, Item 2 and 3, of the Regulations regarding the punishment of anti-revolutionaries constituted by the People's Republic of China, the above mentioned court has, therefore, decided to make the following verdicts:

1. The accused be sentenced to ten years in prison.

2. The seized counter-revolutionary literature be confiscated.

If she refuses to accept the verdict, the accused shall submit to the above mentioned court a letter of appeal and a copy of the appeal to Shanghai Middle Rank People's Court within ten days following the day she has received the letter of verdict.

The above sentence was rendered by:
Shanghai Hongkou District People's Court
Criminal Judgment Court
Judge: Tongchun Chai
Date: November 20, 1963
Clerk of the Court: Xinkang Gu

(Note: It was impossible, in fact, to make an appeal, and if anyone tried to do so, another year could be added to the sentence.)

In prison
The elderly judge who seemed quite reasonable had told me, "You will have a change of environment." The promise was fulfilled on November 23, 1963. Early that morning, along with many men and women from the Second Detention House, I was sent to prison.

Amazingly, I did not feel the pain of going to prison. My heart was filled with joy which overflowed to everyone I met. Even the thief who was sent to prison with me made me happy as if I had discovered some treasure.

As the paddy wagon drove away from the detention house, I was surprised to see brother Wang. We spoke of all that had happened to us since we last saw each other.

That day God gave me the following verses, "I am still confident of this: I will see the goodness of the Lord in the land of the living" (Psalm 27:13), and "The lot is cast into the lap, but its every decision is from the Lord" (Proverbs 16:33). God, the Father, is abounding in patience and love indeed. He warned me before danger approached. He anointed my wounds with His Word to encourage me. Oh, how lovely is the Lord in whom I believe! How can I not help loving Him?

Throughout history many people from all over the world have followed the Lord Jesus. They have trusted Him, loved Him, feared Him, worshiped Him, served Him and spread His name, because He is radiant and wonderful, outstanding above all others. His mouth is full of grace. He is altogether lovely. The length, width, height and depth of His love are immeasurable. The love of God cannot be quenched by water, drowned by flood, cut by sword or swallowed by death.

When I entered the prison, I had to sleep with three others on the cement floor of a small cell, 2 by 1.5 meters. Later, the cell was shared by three of us. To my surprise, every morning before dawn, I could hear somebody singing, "Deliver me, Jesus. Be my guarantee and forgive my sin." For several mornings, she sang, "God is faithful, He will not fail me; God is faithful, never be discouraged," which instilled strength into my soul. I was as delighted as if I had found some treasure. The words of the song were:

God Is Faithful

God is faithful, He will abide by His word.
His promise will never fail.
Your cross, will not be too heavy,
In due time, the cross will be your glory.

God is faithful, He is a reliable Lord.
He will protect you in danger.
Your trial will not be too hard,
In due time, the Lord will smooth your way.

God is faithful, He will not let you want.
For His name is Jehovah-Jireh:
The Lord will provide.

Your every need will be provided,
As long as you offer your praise to Him.

Refrain: God is faithful,
He will abide by His word.
God is faithful, never lose your heart.
If you are true to Him until death,
With help from God,
In due time you will see the glory of God.

That spiritual song came from what God spoke to me twenty-one years before, and I was inspired to write it down. When it was published in the *Bread of Life Hymn Book*, I never expected God to use that very song to comfort and strengthen me when I was afflicted. How amazing it was that God would move a believer to *sing my song* in prison! It reminded me how I forsook everything and stepped onto the path of living by faith. Once again I dedicated myself to the Lord who claimed victory over death by His resurrection. I praised Him for His faithfulness, loving kindness and sovereignty.

Life in prison was full of tension. We had to change cells from time to time and adjust to living with other prisoners. Once I roomed with a prisoner who had a life sentence. She had been the madam of a brothel, had abused immature girls and was very cruel and brutal. When she saw me bow my head to say grace, she reported it to the guard.

The warden called me to her office and criticized me. However by the grace of God I bravely responded, "You are not foot-binding now, are you? To stop foot-binding was what we Christians advocated. How inconvenient it was for older women to walk on small bound feet." I continued,

"Your say your ancestors were monkeys, Ours were not." The warden said, "Do you call names?" I answered, "Don't you believe that man is evolved from monkeys? But I believe man is created by God." Seeing that I talked reasonably, she did not say any more and ordered me to go back to my cell. That day the spirit of joy filled my heart.

Several days later, a Christian in the neighboring cell witnessed my saying grace and was convinced that I was a Christian. People called her "half lung" since she had only a half a portion of her lung left. But she had a whole heart to trust God and was genuinely concerned about me. Unfortunately, she was too weak spiritually to go through the persecution in the political accusation meetings during the Cultural Revolution and committed suicide in 1968.

Usually all prisoners were allowed to go downstairs for outdoor activities once or twice a week. Since I prayed before meals, I was not allowed to go with them. When I asked our guard why, she answered, "It is related to your case." "Hasn't my case concluded now?" I asked. "Why can Buddhists have vegetables when meat is served?" Later, they allowed me to go downstairs for physical activity.

During activity time, I met Sister Q. After I was arrested, she had continued to send out tracts and preach the gospel. She refused to hand in my translation of Murray's *The Prayer Life* and refuted the words of the interrogator, saying that she volunteered to proofread the book. For that she was sentenced to seven years imprisonment.

Amazing is the Lord that He would not let His children suffer in vain. God used Sister Q to lead deeper into truth a new believer who lived next to her. How wonderful is our amazing God!

At the gate of death

My health was of great concern. In addition to my chronic heart disease, I suffered from pain in my right kidney. For more than nine months in confinement at the branch of the *Public Security Bureau,* I had sat and slept day and night on the broken planks which hardly covered the damp, soiled floor. Thus, my kidney was affected. The right side of my belly was bloated, and blood appeared in my urine. Since we had no chair to sit on in prison, we stacked the rough toilet paper sheets to the height of a stool and sat on it to study and work. Only during labor time when we were sewing buttons on clothes were we allowed to sit on benches at a long table.

My heart disease was diagnosed when I was first detained at the *Public Security Bureau.* Only the director knew, and he did not allow me to take any records about my heart condition to the prison. When prisoners arrived in prison, the first thing they had to do was get an inoculation shot. The nurse in charge was also a prisoner. I told her that I had heart disease and could not receive inoculation, but she ignored this, pulled me to her side by force and pricked the syringe into my muscle. That injection made me swell all over my body.

Besides heart and kidney problems, I had a fever and coughed constantly. The antipyretic pill reduced my appetite instead of my fever. Every day, I could swallow only two ounces of rice soup. I expected to die in the prison.

Inside our tiny, windowless cell was a toilet bucket and a big box with our cotton bedding, clothes and other daily utensils, leaving little room for us to live. The cell was locked by an iron barred door, but we could stretch our hands between the bars and pour out dirty water from our bath or washing into a wooden bucket outside.

The cell was far from any window, so the atmosphere was filthy. Sometimes, when the smell seemed unbearable, I would pinch some orange peel to sniff its fresh odor which made me feel a little better. Every joint in my body was swollen, and I was afraid of cold weather. However, on hot summer days I was suffocated by the steam from hot water distributed before dinner for washing our feet. Even in such hot steam, I had to put a thick towel over my shoulders to ward off the chill, and I fanned constantly under my nostrils to relieve the suffocation.

To make things worse, I was always catching colds and continued to be tormented by bugs. One summer I caught more than 600 bugs. Sick and weak, I lay on the floor all day long waiting for death. My heart was like a smoldering wick which might be extinguished at any moment.

In this hopeless situation, praying for help, I asked the prison authorities to let me see a medical doctor. When refused by one guard, I persisted until one of the guards nodded to my request.

To deal with my swelling, the doctor gave me diuretic pills every day. Thinking that it did me no good to rely on diuretic medicine, I asked repeatedly for Chinese medical treatment. God prepared two very responsible Chinese doctors for me. They prescribed expensive Chinese medicine and gave me pills to improve the function of my heart and kidneys. They also gave me cough medicine. For quite some time, I was on a no sodium diet. After almost a year of medical treatment, I was saved from the brink of death by our merciful God.

An evangelistic object lesson

Besides enduring sicknesses and bugs, I was also harassed by my cellmates who bullied me, attacked me and reported me to the guard. Changing cells was routine in prison. Once I was transferred to live with a prisoner who used to be a factory worker. The day following my arrival, she said, "Sweep the floor (cement), which is so dirty." I replied harshly, "I am not a coal ball to dirty the place right away." She was amused by my answer and laughed. The guard came to inquire. I said, "I have a cold and I cannot sleep on the damp floor."

Since the cell was so tiny that it was inconvenient for the others to walk around when one was sleeping on the floor, my two cellmates plotted to throw me out of their cell. It happened that their scheme was overheard by a prisoner in another cell when they were talking about it in the small aisle beside the cell, and she denounced them at the group meeting. As a result, my two cellmates were disgraced.

Later that ex-factory worker tried very hard to incite me to fight with her to give her an excuse to drive me away. One day, when I went to see the doctor, she took the chance to hide my glasses case behind the toilet bucket. After I returned to the cell, it was missing, but I found it later. Still I kept silent and did not blame others.

Seeing that I did not fight with her for the glasses case, that ex-factory worker began cleaning up and made a hole in one of my large-mouthed bottles which I used to pour out dirty water. It was now useless for that purpose. I was already short one bottle which I loaned to another prisoner. It had taken me three to four years to accumulate four such large bottles, which came to me as food containers when my relatives sent some food. In 1968, the privilege to receive food from the outside world was taken away, so I would not get any more of such bottles.

One evening, that bullying inmate purposely kicked one of my bottles and broke it. I still kept silent. But I was somewhat anxious because I would have no way out if she broke my last bottle. Should I report it to the guard? I would not feel comfortable doing so because it was not a proper thing for a Christian to do. But if I did not report it, she might break my last bottle, and then what should I do? So I talked to myself, "It seems that my glasses case can walk and walked away to the toilet bucket. It seems that my bottle can fight and has made a hole in itself." That bullying woman went right away to report me to the guard. The guard came to see me. I said to the woman, "I thought it too trifle a thing to bother the guard. Now it is you yourself who reported it." The guard asked why I said that the bottle had fought. I showed her the bottle with a hole in it.

Later the woman tried to damage my enamel wash basin. Fortunately, the wash basin was very thick. So she only managed to break some chips of enamel from it without leaving a hole in it. Then the Holy Spirit taught me that I should not worry about these things as long as I handed everything to the Lord, big or small. The Lord is just, and He must render justice for me.

One evening my antagonistic cellmate broke her only large bottle carelessly. At the moment when she was in great need, the Holy Spirit moved me to give her a bottle which had been returned to me. Through that bottle we reconciled.

Meanwhile, my health was getting better. I did not need to lie on the floor all day long and began walking around. I prayed for an opportunity to witness to her, since only God's love can melt a stony heart like hers and make it soft.

Time to share the gospel came eventually. One day when another inmate who was in charge of group labor went out, I seized the opportunity to tell her about salvation in Jesus Christ. Praise the Lord! She was eager to know the truth and willing to accept Jesus as her Savior.

One night, the warden came to our cell when I was talking to her about the creation of God from an article about the movement of the cosmic bodies. The warden asked, "What are you talking about so recklessly?" I repeated the saying about the movement of the heavenly bodies. Without a word, the warden turned and left. It is said in Proverbs: "When a man's ways are pleasing to the Lord, He makes even his enemies live at peace with him" (16:7). Now not only did I live at peace with her, I preached the gospel to her and she accepted it. All this was done with the power and blessing of God.

Beaten and punished

In the prison one could buy some daily commodities. Sometimes the labor reform prisoners would come to ask, "Do you want to buy *Mao's Selective Words*?" In Shanghai dialect, the pronunciation of *Mao's Selective Words* and "knitting wool" were the same. Besides, we did not know what *Mao's Selective Words* was. We thought that they were talking about knitting wool. As we had no money to buy wool, we paid no attention to it.

It was quite a while before we understood that *Mao's Selective Works* meant books consisting of Communist Chairman Mao's writings, a set of four volumes. The warden wanted us to study politics. So I borrowed the books from others and read part of them, from which I learned something about the struggles between the Kuomintang Party and the Communist Party.

During the Cultural Revolution, Lin Biao, a high political figure during the early days of the Cultural Revolution, initiated the making of the badge of Mao Zedong, the top leader of the country. The badge was also called "Precious Badge." The government called all working people to wear such a badge. That was not enough. They had to sing the song, *Red in the East,* praising Mao, comparing him to the rising sun and exalting him as the savior of the Chinese. They also had to read the quotations from Mao, ask for instructions in the morning and make reports in the evening before Mao's portrait. When they were buying the quotations or selective words of Mao Zedong, the prisoners were not allowed to say "buy." They had to say "request" instead.

In December of 1968, I heard that the people downstairs in prison had to bow before Mao's portrait two times a day, read his quotations, sing the song "Red in the East" and call out slogans at the end of the ritual. While they were calling slogans, they raised their arms in salute. I considered it was the same as worshiping an idol to bow down and confess before the portrait. I could not do that. However, every prisoner was obligated to observe the rite and worship the portrait twice a day.

It was a lengthy spiritual battle. Unless I received strength from God, I would not have been able to face it. The only way to get strength from above was to pray. So I prayed, "Lord strengthen me for your own name's sake. I prefer to die for you. But never let me bow before the portrait and confess to it. Father, You must give me strength to stand firm." It was not until then did I understand the meaning of "For His own name's sake" in Psalm 23:3.

I felt that I did nothing for the Lord and it was a shame to meet my Lord empty-handed. I prayed that the Lord would act for His own name's sake. What a shame it would be to His name if I could not glorify Him as His child. I felt that I had no righteousness at all before God. I could only pray like the tax collector, "God, have mercy upon me." I wrapped myself up in my quilt and prayed for a whole night. Then God gave me His command of His Word:

"The people who know their God shall be strong and do exploits" (Daniel 11:32).

Things happened just as I expected. December 25, 1968, we prisoners on the third floor were forced to confess before the portrait. Almost all the inmates on that floor were declared "anti-revolutionary," "landlord" or "murderer" and received severe penalties. The few who were criminal offenders for speculating and profiteering were doing outdoor labor such as washing clothes, carrying toilet buckets downstairs, cleaning them, and bringing hundreds of meal containers upstairs to distribute to each cell. However, nobody could escape from confessing before the portrait.

At first, I tried to hide in the back row. That was impossible. On the second day, we had to stand in ranks according to our height. Then God reminded me of Daniel's three friends, Shadrach, Meshach and Abednego, who did not bow to the image of gold made by King Nebuchadnezzar when he commanded all people to worship it. Thus, with strength from the Lord, I stood before the portrait and neither sang nor bowed. All I did was raise my hand when shouting, "Long live Chairman Mao."

After the rite, the whole group descended upon me. They stripped off my quilt pants and lashed me with great force. Some took off their shoes to beat me with the plastic soles. Others plucked out my hair, cluster after cluster. A few days later, they cut my hair unevenly to make me look like neither a man nor a woman. Anyway, I could not see myself because there was no mirror in the prison. It was amazing that I had asked someone to make a cap for me just that previous Sunday before they cut my hair. When I saw other people making caps, I decided that I should have one. Before they cut my hair, the Lord had already prepared a cap to be used in time. His amazing work is beyond measure.

Cutting my hair did not satisfy them. I was ordered to stand and bow before the portrait every day, even during the holidays. Before other prisoners started their labor, I was ordered to stand and bow to the portrait; but I only stood in front of it and firmly refused to bow. Sometimes the prisoners in my labor group wanted to please the guards and came to press my head and force me to bow, but they eventually had to leave me alone with my head held high because they were afraid of the outcome if they spent too much time on me.

Did I stand there alone? No! I was not alone. My dearest Lord Jesus was with me, the One who was wounded and crucified for our iniquities and was risen from the dead. He, too, was ranked among the criminals. I kept intimate communication with Him and continued to taste the sweetness of His presence. When I stood there, the Lord reminded me of the school song of *Mary Vaughan High School*, "To serve Christ is real freedom . . . to soften the hardened with grace."

One morning, the warden of the prison came to me and took off my glasses. She asked, "Why do you close your eyes?" Then she put my glasses on a board and left. I went to put on my glasses again and continued my prayer with my dearest Lord Jesus.

Another time, a guard came to beat the back of my head and ordered me to bow my head. Still I resisted firmly. It was not that I was strong enough to resist, but the power of the Holy Spirit sustained me. Sometimes, the head of the group would beat my head with the handle of a mop. God protected me from serious harm. Thus I stood before Mao's portrait from December 26, 1968 to May 1969.

Due to the change of policy, the head of my labor group told me that I no longer needed to stand before the portrait. Later, they took away the portrait from the wall.

Jesus said, "If you have faith as small as a mustard seed, you can say to this mountain, 'Move from here to there,' and it will move. Nothing will be impossible for you" (Matthew 17:20). Such faith was totally from God. That spiritual battle lasted for several months and ended with God's victory.

There was a nurse in my indoctrination group who used to be a Christian and whose father was a pastor of a Congregational church. She was imprisoned for writing an anonymous letter against birth control. Actually, she was single and did not do so for personal benefit. Since she was labeled Rightist before that letter, she was severely punished for it.

When she entered the prison and saw people were persecuted for closing their eyes to pray, she did not close her eyes to pray before man. She might have thought that it was wrong to bow before Mao's portrait, but she dared not disobey. So she closed her eyes when bowing before the portrait. However, her behavior was noticed from the reflection of the framed glass on the portrait. When other people beat me up, she wanted to be part of that crowd but the guard did not allow her. The guard thought that she was not qualified to beat me when her own stand did not change.

Not long afterward, she became the target in a political accusation meeting for closing her eyes when bowing before the portrait. Besides, she was too careless when talking with others. Because she talked with sarcasm, the group spent more than twelve days criticizing and torturing her in a series of political accusation meetings.

Protected by the Lord, I kept silent and seldom talked in the group, neither in the indoctrination class nor in review. When people asked why, I said, "When I speak more than three sentences, I cannot help talking about 'my profession'—I have nothing to talk about except for my religion. When I talk about my religion, you say that I am emitting poison." After that they did not urge me to talk.

The only occasion when I would speak in the group was during the annual review of the progress in one's reform for the whole year. I would say a few words for the sake of justice if I felt moved by the Lord to protect those who where receiving unfair assessment. Because I seldom spoke, they gave me a nickname, "The Dead." That nickname sounded good to me. I did have to die with the Lord and face the world with death. Every time, when I heard them call me "The Dead," I would say to the Lord from the depth of my heart, "Lord, I have not died totally. Help me to die thoroughly." When they called me "The Dead," I would say smilingly, "I am a heavenly treasure." Although I was often called names and abused, my heart was filled with joy.

Someone pinned several holes on Mao's portrait inside the book of *Mao's Quotations* and had three years imprisonment added to their sentence. Another prisoner subscribed to a newspaper which often carried printed portraits of Mao. One day she unintentionally used the newspapers as a cushion and sat on it. As a result, she was beaten up in almost every indoctrination meeting and forced to carry a poster on her back for many days.

A slogan during the Cultural Revolution, "Down with everything, check up everyone," meant that no one could escape being checked. Everyone had to make a thorough confession and report everything. Another slogan was "Struggle cruelly and attack relentlessly." The struggle not only touched the soul of the people, but the flesh of quite a number. Even worse, a lot of innocent people were tortured to death.

Someone wanted to frame me by saying that I pinned the portrait in the book of the quotations from Mao with a nail. However, my God, who was taking care of me day and night warned me to write down my prisoner number and the date I received the books right on the books and always watch over them so that they would not be damaged by others. The person who brought false accusation against me urged the guard to check my copy of *Mao's Quotations*. But the guard found the portrait was not defaced, thus she could say nothing against me.

Was it not the protection of my wonderful God, who looked after me in secret? Alleluia! Glory to the Lord!

Chapter 7

Surging Waves of Evil

My old father

My father was an untiring learner. When I was in school, he worked in an insurance company. In those days, he liked to order Christian publications, but he did not study the Bible. He loved classical literature very much and often brought rare books home. He was also very interested in Chinese medicine. Some patients whose complicated symptoms of illness perplexed doctors were cured by my father. Therefore, he was very popular with patients.

In 1952, at the age of seventy-one, father received an invitation from *Zhejiang Hangzhou Culture and History Research Institute* to work as a researcher there. While working there, he lavishly spent his income on books and paintings.

My eldest sister never told father about my arrest and imprisonment. All along, he thought that I was in some political indoctrination class and never knew that I was confined within prison walls. In 1964, I wrote to my eldest sister, asking her to change my lodging for some housing in the neighborhood of a park. I had hoped father would then move to live in Shanghai, but my sister did not ask him about it because she thought my plan would not work.

Beginning in 1965, the authorities of the prison asked all the prisoners to work to meet the needs of the government. We bound notebooks, sewed buttons, stripped aluminum foil, made cotton padded trousers, unraveled useless knitted cloth, etc.

At first, our guard asked me to sew buttons. I told her that my eyesight was too poor to do it properly. I did not want to do that job because to focus my eye on such small holes under dim light would certainly harm my eyesight, but the guard insisted. So I did it. However, I could not do it well, so the guard voluntarily changed my job.

When doing jobs which did not demand concentration, I could talk with my Lord in my heart. The inspector suggested that I translate novels. But I thought that if I followed his advice, my mind would be possessed with the contents of the story, thus hindering my communication with the Lord. So I preferred to do something that did not demand too much mental labor; then I would be able to spend more time with my Lord.

Prisoners who did labor were given two or three yuan of pocket money a month. Some prisoners put aside the money and sent it home eventually. Thinking that my father was alone in Hangzhou with no one around to wait on him, I sent ten yuan to my eldest sister and asked her to buy a chicken, have it cooked and send it to father. Before my imprisonment, I customarily sent him a cooked chicken during Chinese New Year. This time my sister did not do as I wished. She only sent the ten yuan to him from me.

By the end of July 1966, father sent me a letter, asking me to visit him for a few days as he had already prepared room for me. He also said that the ten yuan I sent him were "more valuable than 10,000 ounces of gold, which should eventually be returned to its original owner." It was a pity that the letter was destroyed when my cell was ransacked by the guard. It was father's last letter to me.

The summer of 1966, when the Cultural Revolution began, the weather was abnormally hot.. To destroy old culture, old customs, old ideas and old habits was advocated by the movement. My father's collection of ancient paintings was designated to be destroyed. Father used to be an optimist, but I could imagine that he must have been keenly grieved to know that ten cases of his most treasured Chinese paintings—the precious heritage of our country— were doomed to destruction.

How could father survive the intense heat? This aged man of eighty-five did not pay much attention to his own nutrition, and there was no one to take care of him. While enduring the hot summer days in prison, I was reminded of the hot weather in Hangzhou, which was much more unbearable than in Shanghai. All I could do was pray for him.

By August, father suffered a stroke under the pressures from the weather and the political movement. He was struck by apoplexy. His neighbors sent a telegram to my sister. Fortunately, my nephew just came back from Tianjing to visit his parents, so he went straight to Hangzhou to accompany my father to Shanghai. When they reached Shanghai, father wanted to walk out of the railway station by himself, but he could not move his feet. And he could not control the trembling of his hands when he had dinner in my eldest sister's home that evening.

The following day, August 6, 1966, a small amount of phlegm stuck in his throat, and father could not speak. My eldest sister sent him to the hospital. However, all measures proved ineffective and my father passed away in peace.

The *Culture and History Research Institute* in Hangzhou mailed his salary and a sum for his funeral, but my sister politely refused to accept the money because she thought she could cover all the expenses from my father's account. His valuable books had already been donated to *Zhejiang Provincial Library* by father himself. The remaining ones were sorted out by the Residents Committee for more donations to the Library. Later my eldest sister sold my father's furniture and deposited the money in the bank.

When the prison received the news about my father's death, the guard concealed the news from me. She was afraid that I would grieve at the news. During these years of imprisonment, whatever I needed was brought to the prison by my eldest brother-in-law. Although not a Christian, he was willing to help me. He still remembered how I gave his second daughter the medicine which she badly needed for her illness.

When I established the orphanage, he made great effort to support me both with finances and in manpower, showing his enthusiasm for charity. On the other hand, my eldest sister was a principal of an elementary school, and she was always too busy to look after me. Besides, to help a prisoner, an anti-revolutionary like me, would mar her image in the school. Considering this, I did not expect that God would move my eldest brother-in-law to be the one to send me necessities when I was in prison.

Although he was already seventy-eight years old, he volunteered to make the long trips to carry things to the prison for me, which was really not an easy thing for him.

When my father passed away, he brought the news to the prison, hoping that the guard would let him meet me, but his request was turned down. I could not meet him because he was not my direct relative.

Not long after, my eldest sister wrote and told me the sad news. I took the opportunity to fast and pray for my own future. The following day, a young guard called me to her office to comfort me. She urged me to eat and gave me four days leave.

A political accusation meeting

Our daily schedule was to labor in the morning and attend indoctrination classes in the afternoon. During those classes, we assembled in the hall for a big meeting or met in groups to read *Mao's Selective Words,* memorize the "Three Old Articles" from *Mao's Selective Words,* or listen to a speech, and then give our personal responses.

In general, all the prisoners would follow whatever the guard said, and nobody dared express a personal opinion. If someone raised a different point of view, he or she would be in trouble. Such indoctrination sessions were so dull that one's mind eventually turned into a robot. In essence they said that everything bad belonged to the capitalist class and everything good to the proletariate.

One afternoon the person I knew who used to work in the YMCA stood up to strongly oppose God in the class. She was told by some new prisoners about the situation outside the prison and declared that all the churches were now turned into factories or canteens and that Bibles and hymnals were burned. She said to the group, "There is no church, the Bibles have been burned. Where is God? However, there is still someone among us grasping tightly to God!"

To think that she had earned a generous salary and many privileges for scores of years from a Christian organization and now talk like that. I was sick to hear her say such words in this time of difficulty. I could not keep silent and retorted, "Churches are closed, the Bibles are burned, but God still exists!" As a result I was pulled to the stage by the group leader and was criticized and tortured.

My cellmate, the lifelong prisoner, even came to beat the left side of my head. The group ordered me to lower my head as a sign of submission. I refused. They pressed my head down and made me bow by force. I resisted. In the end, I lay on the floor. The crowd swarmed forward and beat me fiercely, asking if I would pray again. I answered, "Yes, I will." They continued to torture me, asking the same question. I replied the same. They beat me until my legs were covered with bruises, asking me repeatedly whether I would pray again. With strength from the Lord, I answered firmly, *"Yes, I will pray."*

It was almost time for supper. When the group saw a guard come from the office, they stopped. I managed to stand on my feet and say to the guard, "I will forgive them for the sake of Jesus Christ." When I entered my cell, I walked over the meal container of the lifelong prisoner. The Holy Spirit whispered in my heart, "I desire mercy, not sacrifice." So I confessed my sin to the Lord.

When I sat down, a clot of blood dropped from my left ear. I suffered from otitis media, caused by dirty water entering my ears while all prisoners were taking a shower together. When people were jostling for hot water, dirty water would splash into my ears and remain there, causing an ear infection.

When I found the affected ear emitting blood and pus, I went to see the doctor. The doctor gave me no treatment other than applying some mercurochrome. Eventually, the blood and pus had formed a hard lump inside the ear which I was unaware of. Now the hard clot had been expelled under the heavy stroke from the lifelong prisoner. When I saw the clot, I praised God, my Heavenly Father. If she had not struck me with such force, the lump would not have come out of my ear.

Romans 8:28 declares: "All things work together to do good for those who love God." The promise of this verse proved valid. I was tortured every afternoon during indoctrination classes for a whole week. In the political accusation meeting, Li Yuan Ru, Watchman Nee's coworker, asked me, "Who is Chairman Mao?" I answered, "He is the leader of our country." She added, "Is he the Savior?" I paid no attention to her. She did not give up, "Is our socialist country good?" I said, "It is good as well as bad." She asked what was bad. I said, "It is bad because I am beaten up."

Later the prisoner who used to work at the YMCA found an article about the theory of the sun in a newspaper. She read it for a long time and then asked me, "What do you think about it?" I said, "Theories will change, law will not. What you are reading about is theory, not law." Then I talked about Thomas Edison, the scientist who invented electric lights, electric appliances, the telegraph, etc. He was also a very pious man. When people applauded his success, he said humbly, "It is God who created these things. All I did is to place God's creation in your sight."

I then talked about Sun Zhongshan, who was called "a great revolutionist and veteran of revolution" by Mao Zedong and Zhou Enlai. Sun was sent to a jail in London through the scheme of the Qin government in cooperation with the government of Great Britain. He fasted three days and nights in the prison. Then he wrote a note and asked the black man who brought him his daily meals to deliver the note to his teacher Kang Deli. Kang published his case in the newspaper resulting in Sun's release.

I also testified how I met the devil at home when I was a senior in high school. At midnight of a Saturday, the devil came to play with the chair beside my bed on which I placed a kerosene lamp. The devil kept pulling the chair back and forth until I woke up. I did not know about exorcism then, so I hid myself under my covers and prayed hard. About an hour later, I heard the retreating sound of slippers. The next day, everything was back to normal.

Li said it was a mouse which was stealing oil. I asked, "Does a mouse eat kerosene?" They wanted to find fault in my speech but in vain. In the end, they read a quotation of Mao, "Receive new things and study new issues," trying to force me to submit. My answer was that "I can receive the good and reject the bad. As to the study of new issues, I study them all the time." Seeing they could not prevail in the debate, they were obliged to announce that the political accusation meeting was at an end. How could I expect that the political accusation meeting would give me the opportunity to share my personal testimony. Through the power of our Lord Jesus Christ, man's evil intention accomplished God's good will.

Writing three checks

All prisoners suffered under the pressures both in labor and indoctrination classes. The hardest pressure came from the spiritual aspect. Often we heard over the loudspeakers that so-and-so behaved well and was released ahead of time and that so-and-so had abominable behavior and had some years added to his sentence. Sometimes it was announced that so-and-so, instead of admitting his guilt, continued to break the law defiantly and was sentenced to death and executed immediately. Such reports sent most prisoners into a panic.

Everyone strived to be the first to plead guilty and denounce others to avoid an additional sentence. Many prisoners tried hard to make supplementary reports about their unveiled evil actions. The command, "Lenient treatment to those who confess their crime and severe punishment to those who refuse to do so," was like inducing child delivery to expedite the process of confession.

In the prison, the guards had absolute authority. When the prison authorities made a report, all prisoners had to repeat it. Since prisoners could not question a report, lying in the indoctrination class was common in prison, as also in society. Lying kept one from getting into trouble, but being honest required courage to accept the consequences.

When a person disagreed with a guard, the whole group would not let go of the dissident until they recanted. Everyone had to be very cautious in speaking. If they disclosed their real thoughts, they would be reported to the guard promptly, with all kinds of trouble following. Besides self-criticism, the prisoner would receive a guilty record of expressing reactionary speech in their annual review.

In our indoctrination class was a prisoner named "Fatty," serving a life sentence for being a member of a criminal gang. She admitted to having hurled abuses at Mao Zedong. She used the similar sounding term "Bamboo Tube" to refer to the name of Mao Zedong, saying "Bamboo Tube, Bamboo Tube. Chop the tube into two hollow ends. May it pass summer, not winter." That was a curse to Mao, a severe crime which frightened everyone. In such terror and tension, I had to rely on my God to advance step-by-step cautiously.

The purpose of political indoctrination was to change our ideology through "brainwashing." Once we were asked to write "Three Checks": to check the original motive of our crime; to check the root of the social class that we belonged to; and to check our social relationships. Through the "Three Checks" one should criticize oneself bitterly, including one's family and any people one had contact with.

The Holy Spirit gave me strength to use the opportunity to write the truth about my father and to reflect upon the root of my social class. First, I wrote that my father worked for an insurance company. He refused to work for the Japanese during the Anti-Japanese War. In 1950, he presented several truckloads of books bought with his salary to *Zhejiang Provincial Library.*

Second, I wrote the stories of two missionaries who set up a refugee camp in Hangzhou during the Anti-Japanese War. I did not mention their names and mission boards, but only described their work and their love. I recounted how a missionary from New Zealand rescued many young women at the risk of her own life, so that they would not be violated by the Japanese soldiers, and how she saved eggs from her own diet for the babies who did not have enough nutrition.

Third, I also told the story of an elderly English missionary, how he traveled to Mogan mountain area risking his life to rescue young men and women. Within a few months, tens of thousands came to his refugee camp, which could hold more than 3,000 people. In the camp almost every meal was free of charge. However, the elderly missionary ate only red bean curd, which was reported to us by his non-Christian cook, who called the missionary an "Old Fool." That was the original motive of my crime and the influence I received from my social contacts.

Finally, I wrote my own story, of how I established the orphanage and housed orphans and waifs whom no one cared about, and I gave piano lessons to poor students without charging them. The guard came to me and said, "We asked you to write your bad side, but you write all in favor of yourself." I told her that we should seek truth from facts, and what I wrote was true about me. For years, God often reminded me of His Word to comfort me when I was attending those political studies. If I intended to please man, God would surely discipline me with His rod.

In some special study sessions, we were ordered to write denunciations against other people. It was an opportunity to expiate one's own crime by such good deeds. In those times, God would remind me of two verses: "Am I now trying to win the approval of men or of God? Am I trying to please men? If I were still trying to please men, I would not be a servant of Christ" (Galatians 1:10); and "Lord, to whom shall we go? You have the words of eternal life. We believe and know that you are the Holy One of God" (John 6:68-69).

I was also reminded of how our high school teacher asked me to color a picture of Stephen when he was dragged outside the city of Jerusalem. I thought that it was now time for me to sacrifice myself for the Lord as God planned.

In the midst of various political movements or when facing the execution of prisoners, it seemed I was carried by a hurricane to the edge of a sea with no means to sail over it. At those moments when the waters roared and foamed and everyone quivered in the face of the surging sea, God's Word would come to me very clearly: "Be strong and take heart" (Psalm 27:14). The Word of God filled my heart with immeasurable heavenly peace no matter how ominous the news that reached my ears or how horrible the stories posted on the bulletin board.

God strengthened my faith. The Lord even let me see in my dream how I safely went across a flooded road in a cart. There was a verse which for years had been my strength: "My heart is steadfast, trusting in the Lord" (Psalm

112:7). Also, "Faith is being sure of what we hope for and certain of what we do not see" (Hebrews 11:1), and many other verses which were my ready strength.

Besides giving me His own Word to fight the spiritual fight, God also strengthened me with many hymns. Sometimes the loudspeakers blared, and the people around were making all kinds of noises. In such surroundings, it was hard to keep praying. Then I would sing in my heart.

Singing was also an effective way to win over Satan, the world and the flesh. The Holy Spirit often worked in my heart with the verses of the hymns. In the evening, when prisoners were locked in their cells and waited quietly for the whistling signal of bedtime, I would sing quietly in my heart, "I prefer to be like someone deaf, dumb and blind, to finish the path in the desert by the mercy of the Lord."

Sometimes I would sing the followings songs: "To be with the Lord," which I composed in 1938 in Hong Kong; "Walk in the Desert," finished in the same year; and "Be Faithful" written in 1942 in the *Bread of Life Church*. The refrain of "Be Faithful" was written by A. B. Simpson. It used to be a song for commencement. I rewrote the main part and adapted the refrain. These songs greatly strengthened me and helped me to survive. Another song, "The Lord Himself" by A. B. Simpson also encouraged me.

Observing God's Word

Like lights in the darkness, the Word of God and spiritual songs shone brightly when I needed them. In midsummer, the cell was like a steaming pot, sultry and suffocating. I felt more dead than alive. However, "He reveals the deep things of darkness and brings deep shadows into the light" (Job 12:22). Although there were three people in my cell, there was usually someone in the hospital, leaving us more room in the cell. I knew it was my Amazing God showing His special care.

Sometimes, God encouraged me through what I read in the newspaper. One day I noticed in the speech of former President Nixon of the United States a phrase, "Immeasurable increased chance," and I prayed, "Lord, how about my chance?" After such a prayer, God gave me a chance.

In our prison, there was a young woman who had heard the gospel and learned to pray from her grandfather when she was six or seven years old. She gave me a note wrapped in a newspaper asking for Bible verses. I knew that I would get into trouble if the guards discovered what I intended to do—there were eyes and ears all around us.

I handed the issue to the Lord and was answered with the following verse, "The good shepherd lays down his life for the sheep" (John 10:11). I thought that I should obey this word with the help of God. God reminded me to ask the young woman to give me back the pieces of paper on which I wrote Bible verses. The girl promised, and I often sent some Scripture verses to her.

This young woman had a forthright character and was easily irritated. Therefore, she often ran into conflict with the guards and was often locked in her cell, but she was very bright and memorized the verses quickly.

One day she was caught by our guard quoting the verses aloud. The guard pressed her to explain what she was chanting, but she said something irrelevant to her question. The guard could do nothing about that answer and let her go.

A few days later, the guard suddenly ordered every prisoner in the east area to leave her cell and gather in the west area. No one could carry anything but a pair of chopsticks and a soup spoon. Hardly had the order passed when we left our cells and moved swiftly like an army.

Only two hours before that order, I had written a Bible verse to the young woman.. So when I was leaving the cell, I gave a meaningful glance to her first and then to a box for waste cotton, indicating for her to put the verse into the box. She did not understand my glance. I became very anxious with my eyes staring at her all the time. It was almost time for lunch when she came to sit behind me. In an instant, she slipped into my hand that piece of paper with Bible verses, which had already been folded into a tiny roll. Praise the Lord that He blinded the people around us and none of them saw us.

With the paper in hand, I hurried to a cell with a toilet bucket in it. There were many people there, some lying on the floor, others waiting for their turn to use the bucket. I tore the paper into tiny bits, wrapped them into toilet tissue and threw them into a toilet bucket when I was passing water. The Amazing God once again protected me. The guard found nothing to be used against me while searching us.

When I returned to the east area, I noticed that the box for waste thread was searched. Fortunately, the verse had not been put there. Otherwise, both of us would have been in big trouble. Our Almighty God led us safely.

The sister who sang in the morning was very lonely. No one from outside the prison came to see her, nor sent anything to her. One day my sister sent me two bottles of phosphate vitamin pills. I gave one to her. The Amazing God once again blinded the people around.

Suddenly our guard ordered all prisoners to be assembled in the west area. I thought they would hold a political accusation meeting to torture me. However, the assembly turned out to be totally unrelated to me. Praise the Lord, He protected His weak child with great mercy and saved me from pressure beyond what I could stand, as it is written in Job 9:10: "He performs wonders that cannot be fathomed and miracles that cannot be counted."

Because of my delicate health, I would catch the flu every time the prison was plagued with it. One day, our guard ordered that all the prisoners who caught the flu be gathered into a few cells. Praise God, I was assigned a cell with a sister in Christ. We encouraged each other with the Word of God and were greatly refreshed when we returned to our former cells.

One of my cellmates was of mixed blood. Her mother had been a maid for a German family, her father a German. They held their wedding in *Shanghai International Church* during the Anti-Japanese War. Now when the church was in trouble, she not only gave up her faith but also accused those who still believed in the Lord.

When I returned to my cell, that inmate proudly spread her cotton quilted bedding so that I had hardly enough room to stand. Instead of asking her to share some space with me, I lifted open my quilt with a flick and shook it again and again. Thus, she could not sleep there with comfort.

She got off her quilt and went to report it to our guard. The guard instantly sent me to another cell. But God was not pleased when I fought with others. He later taught me to be patient, gentle and humble; and let me know that it was not genuine victory to show our temper. God wanted me to die with Jesus, to die to sin, to the world and to myself every day, so that I could live a glorious life as did my risen Savior. It was God who allowed these things to happen to me so that I would be purged and purified.

Sometimes, I was weary with lingering disease and spiritually downcast. I seemed to be struggling between life and death. No light was seen in my misery. Then I prayed,

"Lord, do not forsake me." Praise the Lord that He cheered me up and showed me beautiful pictures of a shepherd and his sheep right through the dirty and peeling walls. He not only made me rejoice, He wanted me to practice what I learned from the Bible, to love my enemies, love those who beat me, even the one who beat me cruelly when I said, "God still exists."

The Labor reform prisoner had a nickname, "Pepper with Taped Head." After the incident of beating me up brutally, she suffered bitterly from lesions on the leg, caused by syphilis, so that she could hardly move around. Later the lesions were healed, but she could not bend her back.

During the annual review, those who had been bullied by her criticized her with one accord. They even distorted the facts and turned the right things she did into wrong, implying that she had done nothing good at all. The Lord did not allow me to attack or abuse her. The Word I received was "to make every effort to live in peace with all" (Hebrews 12:14). Thanks to the Word of God, I stood up to protect her to receive justice.

Later when I was in difficulty, she also put in a just word for me, even before our guard. It is important to observe the Word of God. "The fear of God is wisdom and to shun evil is understanding" (Job 28:28). God let me know that we would fail to be a witness to nonbelievers if we want to please man and give false reports. The Lord says, "Do not speak false reports. Do not help a wicked man by being a malicious witness. Do not follow the crowd in doing wrong. When you give testimony in a lawsuit, do not pervert justice by siding with the crowd" (Exodus 23:1-2).

How dare I not be different in my behavior from the nonbelievers? Even some secular people held firmly to justice because they were reluctant to sacrifice their moral standard for the sake of remaining alive. As a disciple of

Jesus, all the more should I never do anything to gain profit at the expense of others.

It was by the power of the Holy Spirit that I passed through the valley of the shadow of death. With the sword of the Spirit, the Word of God in hand, I kept praying until victory came. If I disobeyed the Lord and followed worldly people, I would lose vigor against the surging waves of evil and its spiritual forces in the heavenly realm, and I would not be able to keep my robe pure without any spots. He is the potter; I am the clay.

Chapter 8

Prison—A Temple of Prayer

Topics for prayer

At the beginning of the Cultural Revolution, Jiang Qing, the wife of Chairman Mao, declared in a newspaper, *Liberation Daily*, "We are dialectical materialists, we are atheists. We don't inherit any tradition of theism." In the pictures carried by the newspaper, we saw that people in society were wearing various kinds of badges. Suddenly we experienced an influx of new prisoners. We dared not ask what happened because discussing our cases with one another was not allowed. But from the confessions of those convicted, we did learn something. People working in science, technology, culture, medicine, education, music and art were attacked as targets of the political movement.

The *Shanghai Philharmonic Orchestra* conductor was sentenced to death. The meaning of his name was related to Gospel truth. I assumed that his parents must have had faith in Jesus. The pianist of the orchestra, who also had a religious-based name, committed suicide with her whole family. Having heard that news, I bowed down and worshiped my Lord. He knows everything before it happens. He did not give me any special gift in music nor let me continue to develop my skills in piano performance. Otherwise, I would have suffered more loss.

To be imprisoned for translating the book, *The Prayer Life*, compiling *Rise and Pray* and praying with other ministers at home, I deemed it a privilege to accompany my suffering Lord. Praise the Lord!

One Sunday, the guard gave us needles to mend our clothes. There I met a new prisoner, who was arrested from Shanghai Jin An District and detained in the district branch of the *Public Security Bureau*, in the building which used to be the school building of *Xiejing Girls High School.* That was also where the *Bread of Life Church* held its first worship service. It was amazing that I learned from that prisoner the story of sister Huang Yiru, the retired president of the high school, since her close relatives were all abroad. However, she loved her compatriots and was reluctant to leave her country.

When we were mending our clothes, the new prisoner told me that sister Huang passed away before the Cultural Revolution; her body was cremated, and her tomb moved several times. Sister Huang had given her good friend Miss Shi 3,000 yuan from her own bank account. It was also said that Miss Shi reproached her nephew for being unfaithful to his wife. So the nephew hated her and denounced her to the *Public Security Bureau* for receiving money from sister Huang. As a result, Miss Shi was detained and confined in a room which used to be her own office when she was the dean of that high school. The sites and names in her story were exactly the same as I remembered.

So I knew that sister Huang, the faithful follower of God, was now at rest in the Lord, and that I no longer needed to pray for her.

Our Heavenly Father is worthy of all praises, for He knew that the tragic political movement was at hand and that sister Huang could not endure the tribulation. Like the Head of a State who sends all his overseas people back home before a war breaks, our Heavenly Father took her home to Heaven. Honor, glory and praises be to our omniscient God!

During the Cultural Revolution, some interrogators from outside the prison came to investigate about my elder sister and several believers. Every time I was questioned about somebody, I received a prayer request from God to pray for that person, and I took the chance to bear witness for the Lord.

One day, some people came to ask about sister Ying, brother Wang's wife, and her sister. They were especially interested in knowing whether sister Ying had joined our prayer group in the evening when brother Bao was at their home. God gave me wisdom to answer the question and I said, "She was nursing a baby and was running in and out all the time. With my eyes closed, I cannot tell whether she was there or not."

Another time, an interrogator of about fifty years of age came with two young girls to question me about sister Huang. With overbearing attitude they announced, "You shall confess who put you up to do such a thing. Denounce the person behind you, and you will be released. Lenient treatment to those who confess their crimes and severe punishment to those who refuse." I answered that nobody forced me. I did it of my own will because I had peace and happiness, strength and eternal life from believing in Jesus, and I wished others to enjoy what I possessed.

I also told them that there is a true and only God and there is also a Satan. Then I described how I met the devil when I was in senior high school. I mentioned that I read the works of Lu Hsun and Bajing, the two famous contemporary writers in China, when I was studying at *Province Girls High School*, but I did not find meaning in life. I often wrote in my diary, "What is the meaning of life?" Only when I got to know Jesus Christ, the true God, in a Christian school, was my heart comforted.

As to Miss Huang, I said, she did nothing wrong. She came to Shanghai to study medical technology and was obliged to drop out because of her poor health, so I invited her to stay with me and be in charge of visitation at the Gospel Center. After the Center was closed, she established a collectively District-owned school in the building of the previous Gospel Center. We also contributed an easel and a bell to the school. I had already forgotten about these two presents, and was reminded by the Holy Spirit when they were questioning me. Then I said that sister Huang had a very simple nature and that I exploited her food ration to support Jiang, who complained that he could not satisfy the hunger of his many children. If it was not for strength from God, I would have died of anger because of such an ungrateful person.

The older interrogator left during my speech and returned later. I guessed that he was telephoning Huang's working unit, telling them that she was a simple woman, not involved in any criminal cases and had no one to incite her for anything. Before leaving, the other interrogator said, "Okay, you are strong! Try your strength with us, the Communist Party." And they were gone.

A few days later, people from Dr. Qiu's hospital came to interrogate me. They asked, "Is Qiu Shaolin good?" I said, "Everyone has his or her own standard for good and bad.

Many people who you think are good are bad to me; many others who you think are bad are good to me. As to Dr. Qiu, he performed that successful surgery for me. His mother was very concerned about me when I was sick and often took care of me. I visited their family after I recovered. Jiang knew that I went to visit Dr. Qiu because he asked me to request the favor of Dr. Qiu to examine his x-ray picture." I continued, "Dr. Qiu is a famous doctor and is always very busy so I simply could not find a chance to talk with him when I was receiving the surgery in his hospital."

They also asked about his relationship with other churches. I said, "I don't know people from other churches and I had no relationship with them. I never try for personal gain by criticizing others. It is wrong to tear down tiles and bricks from other people's homes for your own building." My speech was pointing to those political speakers who, turning a blind eye to the blunders they committed, concentrated on criticizing their dissidents while making themselves to be flawless.

Praise the Lord that He gave me strength to remain calm and composed. I quickly answered all their questions. Sometimes I was even able to argue with them. Fear and timidity, which were part of my nature, totally disappeared. God is amazing who gave me strength and courage to face my enemies.

One day, an interrogator came to ask me about a janitor in the school next to our Gospel Center. People said that she had mopped the floor for the Center, which was not true. I insisted that she did not do that. I told them that there were so many people who had come to worship God in the Center that it was impossible for me to recognize each of them. In fact, I was not familiar with that janitor. I stuck to my story.

There were also two women from my elder sister's

work unit who came to interrogate me. They wanted to know if my sister had arranged to settle matters about her husband's dead body. If she did, she was wrong in her political standpoint. He was sent to labor reform camp because of his political background. After his release, he went to stay with his eldest daughter. Later she retired early because of sickness and returned to Shanghai, so he went to Hangzhou. There he committed suicide because he could not get registered as a permanent resident in that city. Nobody knew the whereabouts of his dead body. My elder sister and her eldest daughter dared not look for it.

Another day, two women interrogators asked me about a couple, the Wangs. I told them my last name was also Wang. The interrogator said that the couple had given me money, which was not true. I firmly denied it. Then they asked what I talked about with them. I answered, "How can I remember? I did not know that our conversation would be questioned." At last, they said that they would come again if they had anything else to ask. I said that they were welcome.

Through these interrogators, God let me know for whom I should pray. Sometimes, God let me see in my dreams that some believers' homes were terribly destroyed. The Lord reminded me to pray fervently for them. It was amazing that I learned later that those sisters and brothers in Christ had indeed undergone indescribable difficulties and misery.

The prison turned into a temple of prayer for me. The curtain of the temple was torn at the death of Jesus, thus opening a way for a lowly maiden like me to approach the throne of grace and pray as a priest for those sufferers. Andrew Murray says, "Be quiet before your prayer and think about what He can do for you and what is your position in Christ." Another servant of God said, "When we pray, we give God a chance." Those were golden sayings that God brought to my remembrance.

A "flying fish" story

For quite a long time, I lived with a young spy from Hong Kong. When I prayed before each meal, she would attack me in order to please the guard. Should I, being cared for and protected by the Lord, stop praying because of her attacks? No, never!

Sometimes people outside the cell would hide my meal container when I was saying grace. While looking for my container, I would praise the Lord and talk to myself, "I don't mind whether I eat or not. Anyone can take and eat it if she wants to." Then the Word of God came to me, "Man does not live on bread alone, but on every word that comes from the mouth of God" (Matthew 4:4).

Other times people in indoctrination class criticized me, saying "You should thank the Communist Party and the government for giving you the meal." I answered, "If I had not had anything to eat before and now I had, I should have been grateful to the government, but I have been having meals for several dozen years. Besides, if it were not for the mercy of God, I would be unable to digest my food. So I shall thank God who is the one who gives me life and breath." They said no more.

Several times when I was saying grace, the young spy would plug into my mouth a piece of very dirty cloth, used for cleaning the chamber bucket. I did not pay attention to her and continued to pray before my meal. However, one day when I was saying grace, she broke the gold frames on my glasses deliberately by force. With the old Adam still living inside, I went out of the cell and scolded her loudly, saying that her father was a drug vendor and she was a spy—but then I regretted what I had said and done.

I reminded myself how Jesus kept silent when He was abused and uttered no threat when He was oppressed at the time of His crucifixion, yet I got impatient for such trifle abuse. The Lord softened my heart by His Word, "For man's anger does not bring about the righteous life that God desires" (James 1:10).

God also reminded me of a story about Hudson Taylor's great-grandfather. One day when he was leaving the factory, a hooligan smeared some soil with bits of broken glass into his eyes. His boss who was walking behind saw the incident and urged him to file a lawsuit against the man, but Mr. Taylor refused. So his boss pursued the lawsuit against that man for Mr. Taylor. However, the man denied his crime. He even vowed that may he turn blind if he had hurt Mr. Taylor. He did become blind not long afterwards, while the eyesight of Mr. Taylor recovered. The Holy Spirit worked in me through the story and I prayed for God to forgive me.

I asked someone to help me fix the frame of my glasses with string. The young spy saw it and came to criticize the person who helped me, saying that the person was not firm in her political stand. I continued saying grace. Then she managed to break the lens of my glasses. I kept silent with patience and stuck the broken lens together with adhesive plaster. When she saw that what she did brought no effect, she began to kick my leg until it turned black, but I made no fuss about it and kept on praying before each meal. Then she started kicking my waist with such a force that I could hardly catch my breath. Still I remained un-changed. What would be my witness, if I stopped prayer just because she beat me? It was amazing that the pain on my side ceased only a few minutes after being kicked, and although my legs turned black, they also soon stopped hurting. I did not report her to the guard, nor argue with her.

She did not allow me to walk around in the cell after supper and contrived many ways to persecute me. I handed everything to the Lord. Then I had nothing to worry about because "The eyes of the Lord are searching over the land. He will help those with His mighty arm who are earnest to Him."

The diet in prison was somewhat little better than that in the detention house. Very often we would have some turnip and cabbage and broad beans once or twice a year. It was entertainment for my cellmate to count the beans in her container, there were so few.

Before 1968, we would have a piece of pork chop once a month. After finishing the meat we would then gnaw and grind the bone with our teeth, wishing to swallow the whole piece. If it was a piece of rib, we would nibble the bone slowly until it was totally consumed. Since meat was scarce in the prison, gluttony was certainly not a problem. After May of 1968, meat disappeared from our meals. Turnip and cabbage were the only dishes left.

On Chinese New Year's Eve in 1970, I took out a can which contained two ounces of pork chop. I bought that can two years ago in the prison. Since then the prison shop had stopped selling food. Usually when people bought a food can, they would finish it right away. I was the only one to keep a can of meat for two years.

I had seen how other people opened their cans by grinding the can on the cement floor or making some holes in it with a nail. That evening, I had managed to make two holes in the can when a guard came and asked where I got the can. I told her that I bought it two years ago in the prison shop. She ordered me to give her the can together with the nail. She scolded the young spy for covering for me. Perhaps she thought the can was sent by my relative, wrapped in some clothes.

When she took the can away, God comforted me with His Word, "You have filled my heart with greater joy than when their grain and new wine abound" (Psalm 4:7). The verse was so clear in my mind that I hurried to write it down in my notebook. Hardly had I finished the verse when the young inmate jumped upon me. She pulled my hair and struck me with her fists, and managed to snatch away my notebook and hand it to the guard.

Two days later, something unexpected happened. In the morning as I was cleaning outside the cell, the outdoor laborer who had been criticized as worthless told me that my can of pork was still on the guard's desk. She suggested that I ask the guard to give it back to me and she would help me open the can. I handed the issue to the Lord through prayer to see how He would guide me.

On that day, each prisoner got two pieces of fried stringfish for lunch and a big piece of fried stringfish and a piece of soybean cake for dinner. The prisoners all cheered up with the smell of delicious fried fish. It seemed ages since anyone had tasted meat or fish. There was no meat on New Year's Eve or on the first day of Chinese New Year. We did not expect such inviting food twice in one day.

At that time, it was not easy for people outside to find fresh stringfish in the markets, let alone for prisoners. At the sight of the fish, we experienced indescribable exhilaration, forgetting the misery of being isolated from family and confined within prison walls.

The fried fish at lunch time did not satisfy our hearts to the fullest. It made us overjoyed to have another piece for dinner.

One of my cellmates was taken to the hospital, leaving two of us in the cell, the young spy and me. I took up the container and said my grace. Then I took a small bite of the fried fish. Seeing the labor reform prisoner was mopping the floor outside, I put down my container and went out to ask her if the guard was in the office. She asked me to go and look by myself.

When I was changing my shoes, the young inmate locked the iron door and seized my hair so that I could not go out. The labor reform prisoner saw it, but said nothing. I returned to my seat and was ready to have my supper when I noticed that the fried fish had disappeared from my container and the soybean cake was much smaller than it had been.

I turned to look at the young inmate and found there were many grains of rice in front of her. I guessed that the grains of rice had dropped off when she stole my fish and swallowed it in a hurry. When she saw that I was watching her, she was anxious and hurriedly threw the dropped grain of rice into the toilet bucket. Then she came to push me on my seat. Gripping my hair with one hand, she struck me with the other. Panting with rage, I went to the seat of the inmate who was in the hospital. It was disgusting that she would pull my hair and beat me after stealing my fish.

When the labor reform prisoner came to clean the doorway, I said in a soft voice, "My fish flew away." Although my voice was very low, the young inmate heard it. She yelled, "The fish flew away?" Another labor reform prisoner in charge of distributing meals rushed up and cried, "Who stole your fish? Haven't I given it to you?" She was afraid that others would suspect that she had stolen the fish. When they were shouting, the guard from the fourth floor came to lock the doors. That friendly labor reform prisoner urged me to report it, but I preferred not to for such a trifling thing. So I stood there and said nothing.

To pretend that she was clean, the young inmate kept pressing me to report. I said, "Since you insist that I should report, then I will do it." To save her face, I chose to report in private, so that others in the group would not hear of it. I was thinking that she was young and I could let her eat one more piece of fish. However, the young inmate thought that I dared not tell the guard because the guard trusted her more than me. She pushed me again and again to report. Finally, I told the whole story in the presence of all.

Having heard what I said, the fourth floor guard locked the prison door and went to tell the third floor guard. When that guard came to ask me, I was obliged to repeat the story once again. At first, she did not believe that the young girl would steal the fish. When the labor reform prisoner reported what she had seen, the guard was convinced.

The note taker next door thought I wronged my young inmate and suggested the guard check the toilet bucket. I prayed that God would forgive their transgressions. In her fury, the young inmate threw all the things from my bag to the floor near the iron door. She even poured out fine grain salt from a small bottle. Things were chaotic.

At that moment, God reminded me to take care of the volumes of *Mao Zedong's Selective Words* that I possessed. In Mao's Quotations provided by the government there was a picture of Mao. If the young girl stealthily damaged the picture and framed me, a new penalty would be added to me.

I had also bought a two volume set of *Mao's Selective Words*, which introduced many policies. If she tore up the books, I would never be able to clear myself from wrong, however strong my argument. So I asked the labor reform prisoner to take these three books out of the cell and put them in a safe place. Being afraid of revenge, she dared not help me.

The guard returned to the door of our cell and in a serious and severe tone she said, "272 (the prison number of the young inmate), however you behave yourself, it is wrong to touch the things of 339 (my number)." In prison we did not use our real names, only the numbers we were assigned. Then she turned to me and said kindly, "339, place well the precious books." I asked where I should put the books. She answered, "Any place that is safe." So I placed the three books under my pillow and went to sleep.

272 was really ashamed to be reproached by the guard. She covered her head with clothes and sat there motionless. From that time, she lost her spirit. Day and night she covered her head and sat still without uttering a word. She no longer persecuted me and ate less and less. She even gave up the chance to watch the New Year's film show which she normally loved very much. I was afraid that her depression would lead to sickness. It would be terrible if she lost her sanity.

I prayed for her for two days, asking God to let the person in the hospital come back early, then she would have someone to talk to. As I had hoped, the recovered inmate returned. I realized once again the great love of God. As it is written in Romans 5:8: "God demonstrates His own love for us in this: While we were still sinners, Christ died for us."

Poor 272 thought that she could persecute me when I said grace. She was seeking reward by beating me, kicking me, and breaking my glasses. On the contrary, she handed herself over to be enslaved by Satan. If it was not by the mercy of God, who let the recovered inmate return, she would have been possessed by the devil and would have become mentally ill.

Although she was saved from the danger of insanity, she lost the trust of the guard and other group members and grew thinner day by day. What a price to pay for a piece of fried fish! She also suffered from pain all over her body, and the painkiller plasters that she applied to her body did not help. I remembered these words: "There is no wisdom, no insight, no plan that can succeed against the Lord. The horse is made ready for the day of battle, but victory rests with the Lord" (Proverbs 21:30-31).

As for me, I received the trial as from God's hand. Through the trial, God trained me to be patient, humble and loving. He wanted me to love those who persecuted me through love from the cross. Instead of hatred, I learned to treat her with mercy. Such an attitude could not be attained by myself. However, with the power from the cross, I could not help loving that sinner suffering from forced servitude to Satan. God gave me the opportunity to practice what I learned from the Bible and helped me to receive it as His great mercy.

Chapter 9

Prepared to Die

A change of guard

During the Cultural Revolution, two new officers came to direct our prison. One was from the Military Control Committee, whom we called Army Representative. The other was from the Workers' Propaganda Team of Mao Zedong's Thoughts, whom we called Chief of Workers' Propaganda Team. Their positions were higher than the warden. All guards and prisoners were under their control and everything was decided by them.

On New Year's afternoon of 1970, they gathered all prisoners in the assembly hall. The Chief of Workers' Propaganda Team announced the prison numbers of those who were classified as anti-reformists, namely those who refused to obey the guards. I was on the list! However, the Chief mentioned my case in a soft tone saying, "339 is an idealist. We do not raise your case to a higher plane of principle."

This meant that I was not accused of an anti-revolutionary crime, so I was much comforted. Then the Army Representative added, "Are your meals or your clothes fallen from heaven?" The Chief of Workers' Propaganda Team promptly went on to another case.

When the meeting was dismissed, the two officers purposely came to my cell to observe my reaction. With the presence of God, I was calm and composed. I joyfully thanked the Lord, because I was labeled as an idealist, which was classified as an internal contradiction, rather than a contradiction between the people and the enemy. The Chief of the Workers' Propaganda Team did not consider it a political case.

In 1970 there were 51 prisoners sentenced to death. Two were Christians. When I heard the news, I could only pray for their families that God would comfort and bless them. On another day, I was asked to attend the death penalty announcement meeting of several prisoners right before their execution. Supported and comforted by the Word of God, I still had peace in my heart.

The Army Representative mentioned time and again that someone insisted on remaining single and was still praying, etc. To clarify my belief, I took the opportunity when the guard ordered us to write self-criticism to give the reason why I prayed. I was ready to sacrifice myself for the Lord if they considered that I was not entitled to live any longer. I would rather forsake everything, including my life, than give up my faith.

In that self-criticism, I wrote, "I often hear the Army Representative mention in the assembly that someone prays. Yes, I pray because I believe God exists. There are four reasons for my belief in God: First, the wonder of the universe and all creation proves the existence of an Almighty Creator whose wisdom is beyond our measure.

Second, some of the prophecies in the Bible have already been fulfilled, some are in the process of being fulfilled and some will be fulfilled in the future, which proves the trustworthiness of the Bible and the existence of God. Third, the experiences of many great scientists and leaders prove the existence of God. Fourth, my own experience proves the existence of God, the experience I had in Christ since I believed that Jesus died on the cross for my sin, is risen from the dead, and that my sins will be forgiven in receiving Him to be my Savior. From the time I was converted, I have peace and joy in my heart. My life on earth is limited; but I will be in my heavenly home forever."

In the prison, we often studied *On Practice,* an article in the *Mao Zedong's Selective Words.* It discusses that genuine knowledge comes from practice and that true understanding derives from concrete practice. Now I wrote down my experience from practice. I handed my report to the office and was ready to die. Since then they never mentioned the word "pray" in general assembly. What a surprise!

One morning, the Army Representative gathered aged prisoners from the women's prison. After a few words, he asked, "Say, if there is God." Some of the prisoners answered, "No God." But I said, "There is God." The prisoner sitting beside me reported right away, "339 says there is God." He replied, "I know, I know," and turned to another topic. The Army Representative was quite gentle and open-minded. When he saw a prisoner beating another one, he would stop the action. Since he took over the control of the prison, fights between prisoners decreased.

God is supreme

God also wanted me to be humble and lowly like Jesus, humble before everyone, whether educated or ignorant, talented or incompetent. Through Jesus, I should be lowly and gentle, without pride or impatience in my attitude and speech.

Ever since 1966, the start of the Cultural Revolution, we had to write on our annual review a phrase, "Supreme Instruction," followed by a quotation from Mao Zedong. God was supreme and I could not rank any man to that height. Therefore, I never wrote the phrase "Supreme Instruction."

Since that formula was designed by Lin Biao, it was eliminated when he fell from power in late 1971. All those who wrote on their reviews the phrase "Supreme Instruction" would have their reviews corrected. I was saved from that trouble.

Before the National Day of 1971, all words from Lin Biao were declared invalid. The badges of Mao and the daily ritual in front of Mao's portrait initiated by Lin Biao caused innumerable people to be persecuted and put to death. God indeed heard His children's cries. The Chinese proverb, "Multiplied evil deeds will kill the doer," was exactly right applied to him. No matter what, Satan still keeps on trying to frame the children of God in every way.

When the inmates heard the Chief of Workers' Propaganda Team call my name in general assembly and the Army Representative mentioned that prayer was not allowed, my cell mates 272 and 67 schemed together to get me into trouble. To please the guards and clear herself from the guilt of stealing my fish, inmate 272 managed to put my bottle of soap powder into the cup of inmate 67. Then she pretended to tidy up things for 67 and took out the bottle of soap powder from the cup. She said that I purposely put the bottle into the cup in order to accuse 67 of stealing things. 272 urged 67 to report to the guard, while she herself was telling tales in the group. Relying on the Lord, I faced their

trick with silence. When 67 brought the bottle to the office,
the guard paid no attention and ordered her to go back to
her cell. It happened that another young prisoner was
talking with the guard and told her what 67 did there.

People said that 67 was very selfish. She had fought
with all her cellmates. One day, a new guard took charge of
the third floor. Prisoner 67 came to the new guard and told
her something bad about me. She wanted the guard to
reproach me so that I would be afraid of her and let her do
whatever she liked. Normally, we each had about a foot of
sleeping space in that small cell, which was about four feet
wide. But the big cotton quilt of 272 covered two-fifths of the
cell, leaving less than one-third of the floor for 67 and me. It
was very uncomfortable to be sandwiched between 272
and 67 and caught in the crossfire.

Prisoner 67 thought that I would be afraid of her after
she reported me to the guard, but I was not. It is written in
Proverbs: "If you falter in times of trouble, how small is your
strength" (24:10). Having heard the report of 67, the new
guard came to the door of our cell to criticize me, saying
"Don't speak one theory and practice another." It was true
that many people who were eloquent with theories did not
observe them. On the contrary, they were double-dealers,
doing one thing to someone's face and another to his back.
I answered, "It is true." I was tired of her endless criticism
and retorted, "Please be concerned about those issues which
can be solved." The guard flung into a rage, yelling "Who
are you?" I said, "I don't know who I am, but I know I should
have one-third of the floor to sleep on." Then I asked her to
inquire of other guards what kind of person 67 was. Thus,
the guard left.

The next morning, the guard summoned a group
meeting saying, "We treat all of you alike without bias.
Don't think that life is composed of trifles. There is politics in

life." Thus, the issue calmed down.

Prisoner 67 tried every way to persecute and irritate me, saying that I believed in imperialism and that an American imperialist was my father. If I had believed in man, I would have gone abroad a long time ago. I believed in God, the Creator of heaven and earth. Therefore I was here, being abused.

I recalled that Jesus was also ranked among the criminals. When He was abused, mocked and crucified, he said, "Father forgive them, because they don't know what they are doing." At the thought of these words, I remained silent.

Storms morning and night

When 67 was sleeping, I was not allowed to touch her, which was hard to avoid. If I touched her, she would back herself up to the cement wall and kick me and push me fiercely. It seemed impossible to lie completely motionless throughout the night.

One night I grew impatient with her kicking and turned even more often. Sometimes I would push her back, but the Holy Spirit reminded me that such behavior did not glorify God. Several days later, with the power of God, I was able to tell her, "It is not because I can win over you or am afraid of you. I am a Christian. For the sake of Jesus Christ, I am willing to care for you as much as possible. From now on, I will try to keep away from you in sleep." Thank God for giving me enough strength so that I could sleep on my side with one leg on top of the other and keep motionless throughout the night.

I remember Jesus said, "Foxes have holes and birds of the air have nests, but the Son of Man has no place to lay his head." Two or three months later, the guard suddenly ordered 272 to change cells. When she moved out, we were attending indoctrination class. Prisoner 67 could not help her. Her quilt bedding, at least five kilos, was too big and heavy for her to carry alone, so I went to help her. I also told her not to stuff the bedding into the plastic bag or it would be torn. I did this for the sake of Jesus, and she was moved by the love of God. Later when she met me in the labor camp in Anhui, she took hold of my hand for a long time and was very friendly. She also informed me Wang Pei Zhen, another coworker of Watchman Nee, was transferred to Qinpu State Farm and died there.

Early one morning, when everyone in a sound sleep, I hurried to get up and knelt down to pray. It happened the guard came from behind. When she saw me kneel to pray, she asked fiercely what I was doing. I recited a verse from the Bible, "Just as man is destined to die and after that to face judgment." In a fury, she opened the doors of many cells and called out prisoners to push me downstairs to the office. There they began to beat me. To smother my voice, they covered my head with a cotton-quilted cap. In that extremely critical situation, I incessantly prayed for help from above, that God would increase my strength and courage. When they pulled my arms to the back and lifted them up, I prayed even more fervently.

As I entered the office, I noticed the huge portrait of Mao on the wall. I prayed that God would help me not to kneel in front of it. The guard asked me to read the first and second lines of *Mao's Quotations*, "The central power to lead our enterprise is the Chinese Communist Party."

Having finished the first line, I told them right away that I had no enterprise. I did not read the second line, "The theory on which based our ideological guidance is Marxism and Leninism," which they did not notice. Then they asked me to read, "The reactionary will not fall without fighting against it." I replied, "People have religious freedom. It is not reactionary." They had nothing to say and sent me back to my cell.

The guard wanted to hold a political accusation meeting against me, but the guard who came to replace her disagreed. Thus, the early morning storm was quenched. It was because my time to go home had not come yet, so no one could hurt me. When I returned to my cell, my heart was filled with joy and I did not feel oppressed by these troubles. On the contrary they were like wings of a bird to help me fly into the clouds right to the throne of the Lord.

A presidential visit to China

In the ghastly prison, the prisoners seemed to live in another world. When it was raining, the gloomy cells were wrapped in an atmosphere of terror. The height of summer brought with it special ordeals. When hot water was distributed in the afternoon and prisoners were wiping their bodies and washing their feet in the cells, they were just like meat buns in a steaming pot. The air was suffocating and the unbearable temperature and humidity made their heads swirl.

All around there were pairs of fierce eyes to search the suspicious and ears attentive to every conversation of other people. The prisoners were like little kids in kindergarten who enjoyed tattling on their playmates to the teacher.

During indoctrination time in the afternoon, the prisoners were seated around a rectangle table like robots, listening to the lectures or studying *Mao Zedong's Selective Words*. There was always somebody to flatter Mao, saying that his words were all truths and that one word of Mao surpassed 10,000 words of other people. The profound boredom of such dry study can hardly be comprehended

by normal people. Actually, it was the strategy of Protracted
Warfare invented by Mao, which placed the people under
permanent heavy pressures. Through intensive indoctrination, people would eventually give in and follow his
theory.

Looking through the windows, one could actually
see the gates of the hospital, where dead bodies were
carried out of the morgue and taken away by trucks. At the
sight of such a startling scene, each prisoner would wonder
if some day he or she would thus end their lives. This
unconsciously added weight to their already heavy hearts.

The prisoners did not know what would happen to
them tomorrow. They were not even certain of their fate
when they got up in the morning. Fear, suspicion, assault,
framing and revenge were boiling in their hearts. Many of
them took pleasure and deemed it an honor to do evil, to tell
lies and injure others for the sake of one's fortune, a possible
early release, as it was announced over the loudspeakers,
"lenient treatment to those who confess their crimes and
severe punishment to those who remain stubborn." Day by
day, the prisoners passed their prison life in an atmosphere
of intense terror.

One day, a general meeting was suddenly held in
the prison. Was someone to be executed? No! Was someone
to be released ahead of schedule? No! The meeting was held
to announce that President Nixon of the United States came
to visit China. The news was a great surprise, which inspired
sweet dreams to prisoners who had nothing to do with
Nixon. Some of them assumed that the day for lenient
treatment was coming. They lifted their hanging heads and
expected that a happy family reunion was near at hand.
Many gloomy faces glowed with smiles.

The husband of a political instructor, a guard in the
men's prison (not the Army Representative or the Chief of

Workers' Propaganda Team), made a long-winded lecture in the assembly hall. He said that the United States had deteriorated to a state beyond control. The whole country was in chaos like the city of Shanghai on the eve of liberation. People were in a panic, shops were closed early for fear of robbery, and there was danger and terror everywhere. In such a helpless situation, President Nixon was obligated to "gather his nerve and come to visit China. Actually, he is a wolf in sheep's clothing. If he does not come, there will be no turning point for the United States."

Those who did not know about the United States thought that he told the truth; but those who had been in that country knew that the guard was like a blind man, telling people something which he knew nothing about. I did not cherish any illusion about Nixon's visit. Instead, I handed myself once again to my faithful Lord.

I was not certain whether I could leave the prison after serving my sentence. I was labeled "anti-reformist" in the New Year's Day for saying grace in the prison, but I calmed my soul by trusting my Lord day by day without any worry about tomorrow.

On the day of Nixon's arrival, the heading on the first page of the newspaper was a word from Zhou Enlai, "Where there is oppression, there is resistance."

After the lecture there were group discussions. Since the note taker often distorted my speech, I kept my mouth shut with an unchanged attitude. Most people repeated the contents of the lecture. Few expressed their illusion about Nixon.

The guard wanted to know what I thought about it and called me into the office. She asked, "What do you think about the visit of President Nixon?" I repeated the heading in the newspaper, "Where there is oppression, there is resistance," saying "I am oppressed because I am deprived of the right to pray and often cruelly beaten up." She asked for my reflection on the speech of Nixon. (I had read the speech once. I dared not read it for long, otherwise people would frame me even worse.) I prayed for wisdom that I would know how to answer her. Then I said, "My comment on anyone depends on what he does, not on what he says. Of course, I hope the American army will leave Taiwan."

Then she asked, "Which do you think is good, the capitalist society or the communist society?" I said, "Each has its bright side and dark shadow." She continued, "What is wrong with the communist society?" I answered, "No religious freedom." She pursued the question. "What is wrong with capitalist society?" I replied, "Corrupted life." She pressed it further. "What is good about it?" I told her point blank, "Religious freedom." When she heard that, she stopped asking any more questions saying, "You are very stubborn. Go back to your cell."

Chapter 10

Preparing to Leave Prison

Accepting the government's arrangement

The years went by never to return. My ten-year imprisonment neared the end before I realized it. Many prisoners would count their meal containers from the day they entered the prison, deducting imprisoned days from their sentence and yearning day and night to be released. I prayed my way to the end, trusting God's care over me.

Before the Cultural Revolution, those who completed their sentences could return home. Things changed after the political movement. Because of employment problems, the prison authorities found it difficult to resettle the released prisoners into the mainstream of society. Many were still in the prison days, months, or even years after completing their sentences.

What about me? I made no plans for my future. It was meaningless to plan. Once again I committed myself body and soul to the Lord.

For five years, I had not even heard from my eldest sister. I had no idea what happened to my rented room and the things in it. One day our guard gave me a form and asked me to write down my plan after release. I wrote, "I accept the arrangement of the government."

Because of dropsy, I ate a no sodium diet for nine months. Sometimes the food smelled so strongly of agricultural chemicals that I just could not finish my portion. However, a prisoner was not allowed to return leftover food. God prepared a stout labor reform prisoner to live in my cell, a peasant who ate a lot. So she helped me finish my portion.

As an outdoor laborer, she had a ration of cold water which she often shared with me. Sometimes she even saved some fish for me. I took the opportunity to tell her the gospel.

Another inmate was not normal mentally and never paid attention to us. Through these seemingly trivial things, I saw my God take care of everything, no matter how big or small. "How precious to me are your thoughts, O God! How vast is the sum of them!" (Psalm 139:17).

The Prophet Habakkuk said, "I will rejoice in the Lord, I will be joyful in God, my Savior. The Sovereign Lord is my strength; he makes my feet like the feet of a deer" (3:18-19). We shall rejoice in the Lord even when we possess nothing. Do we have nothing? No! We have troubles and difficulties. Paul said, "For Christ's sake I delight in weaknesses, in insults, in hardships, in persecutions, in difficulties" (2 Corinthians 12:10).

When I suffered with intestinal bleeding, small skin growths behind my ears and swollen knees, the guard ordered me and some others to do heavy labor cleaning toilet buckets. Twice I was assigned to empty the buckets. As

I was carrying the buckets downstairs, many people watched me closely to see if I was troubled. God's grace was sufficient for me, filling my heart with joy. Another time I noticed that a political instructor hid so she could observe my behavior. She said nothing when she saw me carefully and happily emptying the buckets into the manure pit.

Later some people asked me to carry two buckets at the same time from the third floor to the ground floor. I refused their unreasonable demand which I could not handle with my feeble muscles. They reported it to the guard, who asked me, "Why don't you carry two buckets?" I said, "I cannot because of my infected kidney and swollen knees." Thus, she left me.

When I was cleaning the buckets, a prisoner criticized me because I did not scratch off the accumulated dirt. I answered, "A three feet thickness of ice is not formed in one day." She said no more. Still some were trying to make things difficult for me. They asked me to carry all the cleaned buckets upstairs at one time. Since I was unable to lift so many buckets, I reported their demand to a reasonable guard, who agreed that I should take only two buckets at a time. With the mercy of the Lord, I passed the test of cleaning toilet buckets.

Was everything getting on well? No! Something happened pertaining to the toilet buckets. In the next cell was a young prisoner who hated Mao Zedong. She stole buttons from the prison workshop when sewing clothes at the working board and threw them into our bucket. They were later found when someone was cleaning our bucket.

When that young prisoner returned, she told a labor reform prisoner that the buttons were found in the bucket of cell number 43. Our cell number was 43, but there were also cells numbered 43 on the second and fourth floors.

Besides, my cellmate and I were assigned to disentangle knitted cloth, so buttons were not available to us.

A few days later, the political instructor came to our cell and looked at the name plate. I told her that there used to be a third person who had moved to another cell, but her name had not been removed. The instructor told me to follow her to her office. Then she asked me if I had heard that some buttons were found in a toilet bucket and whether I had noticed anyone from outside using our bucket. I told her that I learned about it when the young prisoner in cell 44 told the story to a labor reform prisoner, and that she stopped her night singing since the incident, which I thought was abnormal. The instructor asked, "When did she throw the buttons into the bucket?" I told her that she may have done it when she carried the toilet buckets downstairs. Thanks to the Lord, who let me notice that before things happened, otherwise people would have thought that I stole the buttons.

After the investigation, the instructor asked a guard to question the young prisoner. The facts were found to be exactly as I said. The case was clear now. The Psalmist said, "In the shelter of your presence you hid them from the intrigues of men; In your dwelling you keep them safe from accusing tongues" (31:20).

In the midst of hardship God gave me a prayer request. In the prison, the hardest thing for an aged prisoner to learn was to rush to the shower room in a crowd. To take a shower was much better than to bathe in a pool with many people of different backgrounds as we had to do twice a year in the detention house. It was easy to get diseases in those big tubs. However, prisoners had to observe a military discipline and everyone must act at the moment the order was issued.

At the order of "take a bath," we promptly took out clean clothing, and with soap and towel in hand, ran toward the shower room. To save time, we would unbutton our clothes along the way, then undress in the dressing room and dash to the shower to wash ourselves with soap. A few minutes later, we had to put on our clothes and return to the cells in a line. Very often we did not have time to button our clothes before leaving the dressing room. Our wet hair would be frozen in the bitter, cold wind and our toes numbed. My big toes remain insensitive to this day to hot and cold.

One day when I was running to the shower room, a young girl rushed to my side and said, "Pray for my future and health." Praise the Lord! He answered her prayer and satisfied her heart! A few years later, she was rehabilitated. She was assigned a job, received recompensed salary and was allotted housing. Truly, those who seek His help shall not be ashamed.

Finally my time for prison release came. A guard from the prison went to my eldest sister's home asking her to take care of me. Because I was still labeled as an anti-revolutionary, the local police station did not agree to have me registered in my eldest sister's resident booklet. They said that since I had my own housing, I should stay there.

My eldest sister also considered it inconvenient. Besides living expenses, she was afraid that I would affect her granddaughter with my religion. Because of my case, she got into trouble during the Cultural Revolution. Thus, I had to wait and join the next batch of prisoners going to a labor camp.

Every time the guard called the names to be released from the prison, I could not keep calm. However the Lord said, "Be joyful in hope; patient in affliction; faithful in prayer" (Romans 12:12). The Word of God calmed me.

In the release group

Nine more months passed since the completion of my sentence. Still I knew nothing about my future. All I could do was to wait patiently for God's sovereign guidance.

All prisoners who were ready to leave the prison lived in one big cell on the fourth floor, with a prisoner in charge. That prisoner used to work in a factory. These prisoners awaiting leave were to write a review about their reform in the prison. In this review they could make suggestions for further improvement.

One of the prisoners was named Shen. As the note taker of my indoctrination class, she had tried hard to make things more difficult for me. Later she lost that position because she wanted to have a woolen sweater of another prisoner and exchanged notes with her. When this was discovered, she was locked up in a special cell. Should I take the opportunity for revenge? No, I would not do it for the sake of the Lord. She was amazed that I would be so tolerant. On the contrary, I helped her in her difficulties.

Her husband mentioned to her mother-in-law that he intended to divorce her. When she heard that news, she wrote a bitter letter to her mother-in-law accusing her of giving too little money to her own mother who was raising her son. When Shen showed me the letter, I pointed out that it was inappropriate to mention divorce. Since her husband had not told her directly, it would give him reason to say that she initiated their divorce. Also it was unkind to divorce him because he was sent to labor in the countryside on account of her. Besides, they should consider how much their son would suffer were they to divorce.

I suggested that she should be gentle and polite in her reply even if her husband proposed divorce. If she wanted her mother-in-law to increase her son's living expenses, she should only consult, not argue, with her. It would be better to have a friend than an enemy. She appreciated my suggestion and rewrote her letter. Since then, her relationship with her mother-in-law was much improved.

In the release group, there was a prisoner of simple nature. Her husband had been in labor camp for many years, leaving her son and her in extreme poverty. Several times she sold her blood for food because she had no other income. In the end, she was involved in speculation and was sentenced to seven years imprisonment.

She suffered a lot in the prison because she refused to denounce other people. In those bitterly cold winter days, there was no sunshine in the prison. When I saw that her feet were frostbitten, I remembered how my cousin lost her feet because of frostbite. Moved by the Holy Spirit, I took out some clean silk from my newly padded waistcoat and wrapped her feet for warmth. At night, I took the chance to teach her how to pray. Through the love of God, the bleeding wound in her heart was soothed.

A few days before release we moved back to the third floor. I happened to live next to a Christian who refused to go to the labor camp after her date of release. She was the one who sang my song, *God is Faithful,* when I first came into the prison. I was told that she was unexpectedly sentenced to death two years after I left the prison.

The day to leave the prison was finally near. Everyone in the release group was excited. The guard, who was sympathetic toward me ever since my meal of fish was stolen, came to me cautioning me, "339, be careful when you go outside so you will not be sent in here again."

One of the guards told me to write home for things I should take to the countryside: quilt bedding, a winter coat and a mosquito net for summer time. So I wrote a letter to my eldest sister asking for those things from my rented room. She told me that most of the things were well preserved. Only some books were lost.

My sister sent to the prison a quilt, which was given to me by sister Li Grace several years before. Since the mosquito net I used at home could not be used in the countryside, I decided not to bother my sister about that. As a child of God, if I had a need, I should pray for it.

To my surprise, the warden ordered the guard of the women's prison to give me a mosquito net. He also asked about my further needs. I said that I had none. The mosquito net from the prison soon became my private, inner room and my shelter in the labor camp. How careful and thorough was the providence of the Lord!

Besides our daily indoctrination study, we would talk quietly in our spare time. Those who had completed their sentences were eager to go home.

Chapter 11

Sent to the Labor Camp

Still an anti-revolutionary

The day for my release came at last! Those who committed crimes of theft, robbery, corruption, speculation, profiteering, and adultery were allowed to return home. But political prisoners, landlords, Christians and Catholics had to go to the labor camp. Knowing my uncertainty about my future, God comforted me with His Word: "For this God is our God forever and ever; He will be our guide even to the end" (Psalm 48:14). I was much encouraged by that verse.

There was an unbroken spell of wet weather in 1973 from early February through March fourteenth, the day when our luggage was loaded on the truck. What a joyful surprise to see the sun beaming with glorious splendor the next morning! The sun declared the greatness and triumph of God, celebrating the great day of our release.

In our release group were eleven women and many men. The road was so clean and the air so fresh after days of drizzling. We departed at six in the morning by bus. Like sparrows having escaped from their cage and excited with the abundant supply of food in the free world, the younger ones seemed to be at the gate of paradise after years of being locked in that ghastly prison. They talked loudly and sang merrily to their heart's content. I was relaxed as if soaring on wings in the air.

About one in the afternoon we arrived at our destination, Bai-Maoling Farm, Maple Ridge Branch, Anhui which was the labor camp where I spent the following seven years.

When we got off the bus, we were lectured by a *Public Security Bureau* policeman. He informed us that two women would be sent to a nearby farm. The seven left among the nine women all were wearing a "cap." Wearing a "cap" meant being labeled as an enemy of the people, an invisible label depriving one of political status in China. Six were labeled anti-revolutionary, including me. The seventh was a landlord. Those with a "cap" would be under the surveillance of the masses with no right to speak or act freely as other people. The guard also warned us not to talk with other people. Even when they wanted to talk with us, we should tell them of our "cap." We should be very cautious in our behavior if we wanted to take off our "cap" early.

The next day it rained again. A rainy day brought trouble and weariness. The muddy road became so sticky that one could hardly walk in boots. Several times, I was stuck halfway back to the living quarters. With meals from the canteen in hand, I was unable to advance or retreat. The Bible says, "Give thanks in all circumstances" (1 Thessalonians 5:18). Should I disregard God's will because the situation was too embarrassing? Should I indulge in self-pity or complain? No, I should not. Since it was God, my Father in heaven, who led me to the farm, I should learn to do His will with thanksgiving.

In the labor camp we picked tea leaves, hoed weeds, dug ditches, applied fertilizers, etc. The third day after our arrival, a labor team leader gave us each a hoe and asked us to hoe weeds along the lines of the trees in the tea field. It was my first time to use a hoe. I chose a light one. Having been on a no sodium diet for nine months, I was simply too weak to handle it.

The team leader was dissatisfied with my labor. I told her that I had dropsy and suffered from nephritis. She did not listen to me, telling me in a ferocious tone that I should do my work over again. When I returned to the living quarters, I said, "I am not sold to them. Why do they not let me go and do something that I am able to do?" Instantly, someone reported my complaint to the labor chief.

The next day, the labor chief changed our team leader. The new leader was mild and not very strict. She even taught me how to hoe weeds properly. The chief also let us buy some daily commodities and sweets to cheer us up.

The summer on that mountain area was extremely hot. When the scorching sun was directly overhead, one could hardly stand the heat. In the afternoon, we were all dying of thirst with swollen heads. I prepared a mug of boiled water in my handbag and carried it to the tea field where I was laboring. Soon the labor chief noticed my bulging bag. With suspicion, she asked a pickpocket to check my bag. There they found nothing but water. The chief asked, "Why don't you use a bottle?" I replied, "I have no bottle." That small happening reminded me to pray incessantly. Unless we keep a vigilant watch against our enemy, we will fall into temptation.

In our labor we would compete with one another in quality and quantity. Since I was not used to walking on mountain paths, I fell down frequently. Sometimes I felt that I could not even get back to the living quarters. At the thought of God's guidance and presence, I was refreshed. All heavy burdens vanished and I received new strength.

"God, deliver me!"

One day, our labor team went to hoe weeds about eight miles away. Since I was a newcomer, people on my team did not know me well. They only knew that I had a "cap" of anti-revolutionary and that I prayed before meals, so they dared not talk with me.

One day when our team finished our labor, I went back alone and got lost in the mountain. I climbed a big mountain, then a small one, descending from height to deep valley and then climbing to the peak again. More than an hour passed. I was confused and losing all sense of direction. I tried to identify my location by the shadows from the sun, still I found myself lost in a deserted mountain area.

Suddenly I saw a boy about seven years old in the distance. I called to him and promised him some money if he would guide me to the tea factory, but the boy was scared of me. He ran quickly down into a valley. I followed him and found a young woman about 20 years old. I asked her the way to the tea factory. She pointed, "Over there," and paid no more attention to me. With no idea of my way and no hope to find anyone to render me help, I went out of the shed and on my way again.

I remembered a story about Hudson Taylor, the founder of the *China Inland Mission*. He worked in China as a missionary as well as a medical doctor. To get a supply of medicine he went from Shantou to his friend's house in

Ningbo. When he got to a town near Stone Bay, his servant robbed his luggage and escaped leaving Taylor alone on his way.

Poor Taylor wandered along many broad streets and narrow lanes, beaten by the blazing sun during the day and invaded by chilly coldness at night. After three or four days searching, he was tortured by his blistering feet and eventually fainted away on a grassy bank. When he came to, he heard people talking around him. Taylor was delivered. The Amazing God prepared a mail boat for him and he eventually arrived in Shanghai.

I argued with God, "Father, you delivered Hudson Taylor and won't you deliver me? What is the good to your glory and your name to let me die here? You are Hudson Taylor's God and you are my God. Please also deliver me."

Moved by the Holy Spirit, I cried loudly, "Old Father, Old Father!" It is our custom to call an old man by such a term, and this time I used those words to address both my Father in heaven, as well as an old farmer I saw across the field. Did the Lord hear it? Yes, He did. To test my faith, the Lord had not delivered me instantly. Now my loving Father came to my rescue.

As I raised my head, I saw the old farmer straighten his back from a rice field three or four hundred meters away. He was looking for the one who was crying "Old Father" and came over to find an odd looking old woman with glasses. The farmer asked where I came from and where I was going. He told me to walk down the mountain, through the rice field, and up the opposite mountain to reach the tea factory. Thank God that I had my hoe as a stick to support me on my rough journey, and I descended the hill toward my destination.

Suddenly, I noticed a fierce man of middle age standing beside the road staring around wildly. That made me nervous. I prayed fervently that God would protect me from any danger. Praise the Lord, I calmly passed that man without incident.

Soon I caught sight of our tea factory. When I arrived at the living quarters, everybody had already finished their supper which I missed and was ready for indoctrination class. Almighty God delivered Hudson Taylor in 1856. He likewise delivered me in 1973.

There was quite a distance between the living quarters and the assembly hall. One night when I was returning from the hall to the living quarters, it was very dark. The young people all hurried back to sleep and the lights in the living quarters were all turned off. I had no flashlight. My eyesight was poor. Like a blind person, I was fumbling in the dark. Then I perceived something shimmering in front of me. It reminded me of the pond, so I made a detour. It was God who was looking after me and guided me safely.

In our room, everyone slept on a long bamboo bed. Being afraid to get into the wrong place and make a fuss, I continued to pray for God's guidance. Praise the Lord, He let me find my own bedding in the dark. In my most embarrassing situations, God was always there.

In the production team

In the labor team I met the note taker of our indoctrination class from the prison in Shanghai, the one who had wanted to divorce her husband. She came to the labor camp later than me. Her husband worked in Southwest China far from our camp and was unable to write to her frequently. She was resentful, and the idea of divorce struck her again. So she came to talk it over with me. I reminded her how much her son would suffer from a broken family and persuaded her to be patient.

A few months later, she got into trouble and was afraid to have the "cap" put on her. She took the opportunity of picking tea in the field to tell me what she thought about it. I gave my testimony and advised her to hand over the burden to our Heavenly Father. I also comforted her with God's Word in the Bible. The Holy Spirit worked in her heart and she accepted my suggestions.

After she was rehabilitated, she and her husband made a long trip to visit me. Later she settled in Southwest China with her husband. One day she wrote me a letter saying, "To tell the truth, I have appreciated very much your uprightness and have often been moved by your kindness and generosity since I met you in 1968. Believe me that I am sincere. I never dreamed that you and I would be able to enjoy our lives again. I believe that it is the mighty power of God and the protection of our Savior, Jesus, that delivered us from misery." Praise the Lord that an intellectual like her would write such words, a truly amazing deed of God.

Our production team had a labor force of more than two hundred people in charge of tea fields covering one million hectares. A hectare is equal to 1.471 acres. Most of us labored in the tea fields. We picked tea during the day and attended indoctrination class in the evening. In the field, the presence of God enabled me to hear the singing of the birds. To me they were singing "Ebenezer: Hitherto has the Lord helped us." Some birds sounded as if they were groaning day and night reminding me that the whole creation had been groaning in the pains of childbirth, waiting to be liberated from bondage into the glorious freedom of the children of God (Romans 8:21).

At night, the frogs from the rice fields formed a chorus to praise the Sovereignty and Wisdom of the Almighty Creator. I was most enchanted by the singing of a certain kind of bird, which sang such moving and exquisite music. Intoxicated by their singing, I felt as if I were in a heavenly conservatory of angels performing a symphony with different kinds of musical instruments.

As hundreds of birds competed with one another in singing, I would hum hymns softly. However, the gentle voice of my Lover, the Lord, sounded much sweeter than any other music in my ears. While my hands were busy with tea leaves, my ears were attentive to the singing of the birds and my heart was worshiping my beloved Lord, the Creator of the universe, the Savior of humanity. Sometimes my mind was so concentrated on these thoughts that I forgot where I was. I would linger in the tea field until the guard came to urge me to go back to the living quarters for lunch.

For those picking tea leaves, there was a daily quota. To meet the quota, we labored even when the sky was heavily clouded, and during thunder, lightning and pouring rain. We competed with one another and made the most of every minute to complete our quota.

On rainy days, tea plants grew rapidly and the leaves were tender and heavy. Being afraid to lag behind, I sought to continue my labor in the field. Loaded with a heavy tea basket on my back and wrapped in a plastic raincoat, I waddled on the muddy mountain road with the aid of a stick. My fingers became numb, and I had to pull them straight again after bending them to pick the leaves. My underclothes were always wet with perspiration.

Occasionally, we were cheered by some unexpected discovery. How lovely were these light blue bird eggs nested in the evergreen tea groves. However, nothing could compare with the happiness of being with my Lover, the Lord, every minute. The sweetness and joy in my heart surpassed anything the world could offer.

The four groups of "capped" elements—landlords,

rich peasants, anti-revolutionaries and bad elements—had to labor two hours under surveillance even on holidays. In addition to working in the tea fields, we had to plant trees along with young people. The soil in Anhui was very hard. People called it "iron-plate soil." To plant a big tree, one had to dig a deep hole, then dig out a tree from another place and plant it in the hole. Such labor needed strong muscles, which could not be found in a frail, elderly woman like me. God was merciful. He moved a young man to dig a hole for me and a young woman to prepare a big tree for me to plant in the hole.

Under political pressure, the quota for tea picking was raised from time to time. Long working hours, exhausting labor, and poor nutrition undermined my health. Eventually, I collapsed and ran a high fever with my temperature soaring to 104 degrees. My head was spinning and I fell dizzily into bed.

When others saw that I was very sick, they sent for the practitioner who diagnosed that it was malaria. She gave me an injection and some pills which brought my fever down, but my muscles and bones were aching and I lost all appetite. I felt I was going to die. Then the Lord told me, "You will not die but live, and will proclaim what the Lord has done" (Psalm 118:17). That verse greatly strengthened me.

To please the labor chief, the practitioner refused to give me a sick leave permit because of my "cap" and my firm belief in Jesus. Meanwhile she gave sick leave permits to those who were friendly with her. It was God's mercy that someone who had a grudge against her raised the issue of her unjust practice. She was consequently criticized and obliged to give me sick leave.

One day someone borrowed some money from me, leaving only a few cents in my pocket. It happened that a vendor came to sell persimmons, three of them for ten cents. It was rare to get persimmons at such a reasonable price and someone offered to buy three for me.

My kidneys did not function well and to have some persimmons would somewhat help my urinary problem. However, I had only a few cents left. My principles did not allow me to borrow money, nor press for the return of debts, because Proverbs 19:17 says, "He who is kind to the poor lends to the Lord and he will reward him for what he had done." The Lord also says, "Lend without expecting to get anything back" (Luke 6:35). By no means could I accept the persimmons bought for me by other people.

How to handle one's money is very important. Some ministers and believers fall short of God's glory with money. Should I start to degrade my moral standard through that tiny occasion and eventually follow those corrupted ministers? No, I should not! By the power of the Holy Spirit, I would not do it. As a Christian, my body belongs to the Lord. I shall not follow my flesh and disobey the Lord's command.

Since being transferred to the sick and aged team, my work became much lighter. The guard often sent me alone to the top of the hill to hoe weeds. While hoeing, I was inspired to praise the Lord with a song taught by Dr. John Sung:

> Lord, I believe; Lord, I believe.
> Strengthen my faith so that I can move the mountain.
> Lord, I believe; Lord, I believe.
> Bury all my doubts in the deep spring well.

Sometimes, after laboring under the scorching sun, I would wash my face beside a pond. Then I realized how my Lord restores my soul with His Living Water.

When water buffalo plowed the tea field, big lumps of soil pressed against the twigs of the trees. I would hurry to pull the twigs out of the soil, praying "Lord, I cherish the twigs which cannot save themselves from the heavy weight and pull them out of the soil. I believe that you will not desert me. May you likewise deliver me and set me free. I believe you can liberate me from bondage with your mighty power, because there is nothing too difficult for you." That prayer I repeated time and again. Did God hear my prayer? Yes, God who hears the cry of a crow heard my prayer.

One day, when I was plucking weeds by hand from the root of a tea shrub, I suddenly felt uncomfortable inwardly and was moved to use my hoe instead. I followed my inner impression. A huge snake glided out. With the hoe, I killed it without fear. God enlightened me through that incident to understand that as long as I rely on God with all my heart, I can win over the evil power.

Another afternoon, the rain was pouring down. I was concentrating on in picking tea leaves from a shrub when a long, thick snake slowly slid along the branches. When I noticed it, the snake was staring at me. I was struck by Psalm 121:4-5: "He who watches over you will not slumber . . . nor sleep. The Lord watches over you, the Lord is your shade at your right hand." God protected me even when I was unaware of the threat of a poisonous snake.

During the busy season, people in the production team had to cut rice. To avoid the grains cracking under the sun, thus suffering the loss of harvest, everyone had to start out before dawn. With the aid of the Lord, I went with them, though it was not easy to follow them to the rice field in the dim pre-dawn light. Since I was poor in eyesight, it was hard to jump over ditches and wade across brooks.

My job was to pick up leftover grain behind the harvesters. As I was gleaning in the rice field, I remembered

how Ruth, who was included in the genealogy of Jesus
Christ, had collected grain in the fields. At the thought of
that story, my heart was filled with joy and I spared no effort
in doing the job.

When I was pressed by a gust of strong wind to run
to shelter in a ditch, God showed me that He was my resting
place where the wind cannot reach. In Him I enjoyed
perfect peace which transcended all understanding and
could not be disturbed by man, because He is the fortress of
the poor and distressed.

"Jesus' daughter"

Besides labor, we had to attend political indoctrination every evening. Because I was saying grace before every
meal, someone in the living quarters asked, "Are you dizzy
before meals?" I said, "No, I am very well." She did not know
how to ask further, and I was unable to say more because it
was prohibited from preaching the gospel.

To earn merits, the head of the indoctrination class
organized group members to criticize me. They empha-
sized that it was labor that maintained human life. I quoted
the second verse of a song they were all singing to respond,
"The growth of everything depends on the sun" to point
out that the growth of plants depended not only on man's
labor.

I used a metaphor of building a house to declare the
mighty work of God. I said that when one sees a house, it is
evident that there was a designer and a builder who made
it. It was impossible that it was built or assembled by itself.
Similarly, there must be a creator for this wonderful universe. That was one of the reasons for my belief in God.

Seeing that they could not convince me, the head of
the group invited the top leader, the political instructor, to
criticize me. When I spoke about the creation of God, the

instructor asked, "Where are you from?" I promptly replied, "I was born of my parents, but the first man was created by God." Instead of being submissive, I took the opportunity to affirm God's creation.

They then sent for a former minister, hoping that she knew how to criticize me. When she came in, she mentioned nothing about religion but only of studying *Mao Zedong's Selective Words*. Seeing that criticism would get nowhere, the instructor went back to her office, leaving behind a word, "Keep her under surveillance and criticize her whenever she prays, which is not allowed." However, nobody took it seriously.

One afternoon, the instructor came to me while I was picking tea. She collected a bunch of tea leaves and asked, "Do you drink tea?" She meant to give me a lecture. Actually, I do not drink tea, but prefer only boiled water. The instructor could not pursue the topic further because I was not interested in tea. Thus, she went away.

Time passed more quickly when I was busy every day, and the end of 1973 was near. When our group members came one at a time for their yearly review, a male chief came to sit in our group meeting. Then a person named Pan asked me, "Do you love Chairman Mao or God?" I answered point blank, "God!" The whole room was silent and the male chief was embarrassed.

After a while, the male chief told us a story of an engineer, saying, "There is a hydroelectric engineer in the central farm. He is a returned student from America. When he was working in Shanghai, his monthly salary was over 1000 yuan. Now he has only a little bit more than 70 yuan a month in the main farm. He is an expert and can detect the root of any trouble about electricity by reports without examining it in person. When he first came to the farm, he used to shade his eyes for a while before meals. People learned that he was saying grace before meals. By and by, people did not see him do it because he changed his mind." Then he added, "However, there is someone who is going to see God with a granite-like skull." I said, "It is good to be able to see God. Unfortunately, many people are unable to see Him."

Early next morning, the chief in charge of our ideological reform came and said to a young woman called Zhao, "You knew that what Pan said was wrong. Why did you write it down and repeat it?" Then the guard reproached Pan, "Don't you know her? She will preach even when you don't ask her. Now you have given her a chance to preach by asking that question." At last she asked me, "Is your belief handed down to you by your ancestors?" I answered, "My belief is not inherited but accepted by myself." She added, "Isn't your father a believer?" I said, "My father was careless about his religion. I am different. I am very serious." She left without saying any more.

That month when our wages were assessed, Pan had two yuan deducted from her previous wage because she asked me whether I loved Chairman Mao or God in the meeting of our yearly review. Pan's previous wage was 22 yuan and 90 cents (equal to 11 dollars and 40 cents at that time). My wage was already the lowest, which was 16 yuan and 90 cents including meal tickets (about 8 dollars and 40 cents according to the foreign exchange rate at that time).

On the farm, ten cents was a big sum, let alone two yuan. Usually people spent more than ten yuan on meals and the rest on daily commodities and snacks. Pan smoked. She had to spend money on cigarettes so it was a great loss to her.

The news of my answers to the chief soon spread to other groups and everyone in the team was talking about it. It was common practice in the team that whatever happened, no matter how trifling it might be, it would be known by the hundreds of people in the team immediately. When we had nothing to talk about during indoctrination class, we would discuss what happened in other groups.

When people knew my story, they nicknamed me "Jesus." Some called me "Old Jesus," some "Aunt Jesus," and others, "Daughter of Jesus." Some did it for sarcasm and others did it out of respect. Most of them did not know the truth. Whatever their intention was, I answered all of them with joy. I told them that I was neither Jesus, nor the daughter of Jesus, because Jesus had no daughter. I was Jesus' student. However, everyone who believes in Jesus is a child of God.

One night when I was going out of the assembly hall, a young woman came to ask me, "Jesus, Jesus, why are you so ugly?" I answered smilingly, "I am lucky to be ugly. Otherwise, I would sin more." That young woman was the first to say something out of a sense of justice about my case. When I met her years later in her production team, since I had been transferred to the sick and aged team in February 1975, she said, "Jesus, I thought you had been gone for a long time. A person like you should not stay here any longer because people should have religious freedom. Hurry to appeal to the court."

Life in the common living quarters was not as easy and free as in a family living quarters. People from family living quarters were not under the supervision of others and they were allotted some meat dishes during the holidays.

Someone talked to me, "Jesus, I will find a boyfriend for you from Juntian Lake Farm, a man who has never married, just like you. Juntian Lake Farm was a male farm where life conditions were much better than on our farm. I refused, having dedicated myself to be a virgin, to serve the

Lord with undivided devotion.

I was very grateful to the Lord for being single when I was arrested so that I need not be worrying about family and children. How could I seek comfort now when the spiritual war was becoming white-hot. No, I will say a thousand times no to the proposal.

As to young people, I suggest they marry to avoid leaving a foothold to the enemy, if they do not have any guidance from God. A family with Christ as its head will bear good witness for the Lord. Many of God's servants are greatly used by the Lord because they have pious and godly parents.

As for me, I chose to be single for the Lord when I was still young. Should I change my mind for the comfort of the flesh and get married in my old age? No! To dedicate all my life to the Lord was not to suffer. Instead, it was supreme happiness and a special gift and privilege. Praise the Lord! He is faithful and has protected me by His mighty hand from sinning against Him in affairs between men and women.

Nowadays, many old parents have to move out and give their rooms to their children when their children get married. Once the children succeed in moving into their parents' rooms, they will change their filial behavior of doing their bidding in all things and put on a ferocious face to mistreat them with all manner of evil. Except for a few from godly families, even children of Christian families do not seem to respect their parents, which is contrary to the moral tradition of our country.

The Cultural Revolution has changed China in many respects. Some call their unemployed parents "wastes." When young people are looking for a mate, they would ask, "Do you have a 'waste' at home?" Therefore, many parents envy us who have no children.

Chapter 12

At Last! A Short Leave

God's provisions

I had paid rent for more than twelve years for my house in Shanghai. Although the monthly payment was not much, the accumulated sum was considerable. Besides, I was unwilling to let my eldest sister pay my rent. Therefore, it was necessary for me to settle my household duties.

According to labor camp regulations, only those with immediate family members could ask for home visit leave. Not having immediate family members, I could only ask for leave of absence, which would not be granted until my application was approved by every chief. From a human viewpoint, I was destined to spend the rest of my life in the camp.

When I was transferred to the sick and aged team, the chief in charge of reform told me, "When you are unable to work, you can live on the subsidy from the government."

I asked, "Why don't you let me go home? Mutual trust concerns two parties. It is impossible to ask me to trust you when you don't trust me. I want to leave for a home visit. Why don't you approve it?" She was quite at a loss for a reply. Then I said, "I have to deal with my house and the piano. The woolen things must have been eaten by moths after so many years."

My niece, Zhongchi, had a little son who needed a room where his nanny could live with him. My second sister attempted to change the name of the lease holder of my house to her own, but the people in the Housing Administration Bureau refused her application saying that the lease belonged to me. The room that I leased was small, only about ten square meters. God preserved it for me.

On November 14, 1974, when I returned after a day's labor, someone told me that the guard sent for me. I was granted a leave of absence for fifteen days including the time to and from the camp.

That evening I was as exhilarated as a bird set free from its cage. Many team members shared my happiness. The Lord answered my prayer and moved the chiefs to let me go home. More than twelve years had passed. However, our faithful God never changes.

In the prison theft was common. A good cotton bedding quilt would be exchanged for an old, worn out one. Very often the thieves would take offense as if they were wronged. In the labor camp, theft became more common. However, when I was going home, God prepared for me a very honest peasant who offered to carry things for me. She even took care of my things and helped me get a steamer ticket.

When we arrived in Shanghai, she helped me carry all my things to the trolley bus and had my luggage carefully wrapped with ropes, so that when they were taken off the bus I could easily carry them to my sister's house. It was as rare as a unicorn's horn to have such a reliable companion on my trip.

The moment my eldest and second sisters saw me, immeasurable joy brought tears to their eyes. My niece, who "was lost and found again," confessed her sin with bitter tears because she had denounced me in her working unit and distorted the strict discipline that I carried out with her. That day God let her read Psalm 102:20: "To hear the groans of the prisoners and release those condemned to death." I was much encouraged by the Word she received from God and I prayed with her every day.

The most exciting thing for me on the day of my arrival was that I was well fed by the spiritual food which I had craved for years—the Bible. The verse I read that day was Genesis 17:1: "I am God Almighty; walk before me and be blameless." I prayed that God would give me strength and grace to find favor in His eyes.

God also helped me to obtain the book, *Streams in the Desert*. The author related this story of a window:

> Once there was a very beautiful picture on a window of a Catholic church. One day the window was shattered by a hurricane and everybody felt sad. An artist came and asked the church leaders to give him the bits of broken window. Later, the church members received an invitation to an art exhibition. Among the many works displayed, they noticed a very beautiful glass window, made from the broken glass window they had cast aside. How wonderful that the useless bits could become a splendid picture through the skill of an artist!

Applying the story, the author said that Jesus was the mender of those who had broken lives. This reminded me

that Jesus is wiser than any artist in the world. In due time
He will fully manifest His glory.

Although I knew God's promise that He would grant
me grace and fulfill His work, I was, unfortunately, still
keeping an eye on the circumstances and acting by my own
knowledge. When told that two people in our neighborhood were arrested in a family gathering just two days
before my return, I foolishly thought that I should take
precautions to avoid such an incident.

There were piles of testimony books in my attic,
many of which had my pictures and name. To avoid the
implication of other believers, I tore off all the covers and
tore out pictures from the testimony books and sold part of
them to a recycling station as waste paper. Only half of the
books were preserved. Because of my weak faith, I was
wrong to do that.

Just like an unfaithful steward, I wasted the possessions of God's family. I entrusted all the copies of the Bible
and of the separate editions of the Gospels and Psalms to a
believer so that they could be used by those who needed
them at any time. Because I had only fifteen days leave, I did
everything in such a hurry.

A brother in Christ who had been my piano student
prepared fifty yuan for me to buy things. My two sisters
gave me the remaining sum of the inheritance from my
father, refusing to keep a share. I saw God's mercy and my
small faith. My loving and merciful God did not forsake me,
nor repay me according to my iniquities.

My eldest brother-in-law was eighty-six years old
then. Since he was hard of hearing, I wrote a note to him. I
thanked him for bringing things to me over the many years
I was in prison. I also told him that I often prayed that God
would let me share His salvation that he might receive Jesus
as his Savior and be saved. He had heard the gospel for a

long time, but never accepted it. This time when he read the note, he said smilingly, "I will, I will." God also let me enjoy fellowship with other members in Christ.

Physically I was suffering from many kinds of ailments. God moved sister Ying to introduce a doctor, a pious Christian working in a hospital nearby.

The doctor was very responsible. He gave me proper treatment for my heart and kidneys. He gave me an x-ray and discovered that I had pulmonary emphysema. I also suffered from severe arthritis which did not seem to improve with several treatments of acupuncture. After a thorough examination of my health, the doctor wrote a medical certificate for me to ask for sick leave from the labor camp.

Because of my sickness, I asked to extend my leave time and again. In addition to my fifteen days leave, I was able to remain in Shanghai for fifty days. The chiefs in the labor camp began to worry about me and they sent people to Shanghai to investigate my situation. They even went to the hospital and asked the doctor to issue a medical certificate about my health so that they could submit something to their authorities.

They also went to the local police station to ask about my residential registration. Fortunately, I registered my stay every time I extended my leave so the people from the labor camp could find nothing against me. Thus, I got fifty days medical leave.

Even though I got the leave, the authorities refused to give me pocket money or food coupons. Food coupons were indispensable to every resident, but hard to obtain even with money.

God who heard the cry of ravens and prepared food for them also provided me my daily bread. He moved two of my former students (X.S.E. and X.T.E.) from the orphanage to give me some food coupons. X.T.E. also gave me forty yuan. I was in tears when I received the money. I gave him my only woolen blanket as a souvenir. Another student (N.S.E.) remitted thirty yuan to me from Shandong, and I sent him my father's leather jacket.

The day when I was going back to the labor camp, T.E. arrived at my doorstep around four in the morning and took my luggage to the bus station by bicycle. People thought he was my son. Actually, he was better than a son. Some sons draw a line between their parents and themselves and disassociate from them when their parents are labeled as anti-revolutionaries. T.E. did not stay away from me because of my "cap."

He bought a ticket for me and put my luggage onto the bus. What impressed me most was T.E.'s friend, a middle-aged stranger who also came to see me off. Because T.E. was unable to carry two pieces of luggage at the same time, this friend kept one piece in his home and brought it to the station along with a bag of biscuits. I was deeply touched by his concern. It was God's mercy to revive my soul.

In man's eyes, God's plan for me was in vain. However, my broken life was completing God's Sovereign will which strengthened my faith and fostered my spiritual growth.

A precious sister's trials

When I returned home, I found that sister Huang, who used to live with me, had suffered from a mental disorder. That was my only grief. Sister Huang had been working among poor children with Miss Woods, the missionary from New Zealand, for twenty years. Sometimes she accompanied Miss Woods to the mountain areas. Life was hard. She had to do some side jobs to earn her living. When Miss Woods was forced to leave China, Huang came to Shanghai and lived with me for more than eight years. After my arrest, she lived alone and continued to teach in the collectively State-owned school.

Sister Huang was basically simple in nature and plain in life and very obedient to her father. Her mother passed away long ago. Due to her excellent teaching, she was admired by her students and the principal. But when the Cultural Revolution began, intellectuals were labeled as "Stinky Old Ninth," and Christians and Catholics were accused of anti-revolutionary crimes and connections with American imperialists. They were all attacked to a certain degree and tortured and isolated until they renounced their beliefs. Sister Huang was no exception.

Her blood brother could not help her because his wife craved for vain glory. Her blood sister who was a Christian lived in Hangzhou and was unable to maintain contact with her. When the Red Guards took away her Bible, she was too scared to pray any more. She was even afraid that her neighbors would persecute her more cruelly when they found her praying. Thus she was discriminated against and despised at school and bullied and wronged by her neighbors at home.

Sister Huang was physically weak because of malnutrition, and the political pressure laid a heavy load on her mind. However, she did not hand over her burden to the Lord. The heavier the pressure, the more suffering she felt, and the more scared she became. In the end she collapsed and became mentally disturbed.

When I returned from my sister's home, I went to her room and gave her some silk clothes. I asked if she prayed alone or read the Bible. She did not answer me, but had a fit, speaking nonsense and making all kinds of gestures. The alarm clock that I gave her when I was arrested was broken to pieces during one of her fits. She also had hallucinations and would say there were many snakes in the basin she used for foot washing. I felt very sad.

Satan tried to trap her in many ways. He made her feel that life was nothing but torture, so she tried to cut her own throat with a pair of scissors. By the mercy of God, she was discovered in time and sent to the hospital. She survived after emergency treatment. That incident was at the beginning of the Cultural Revolution.

Since I was still labeled as anti-revolutionary, and she was an honorably retired teacher, to avoid getting her into trouble I dared not speak too much with her. I wanted to talk with her cousin who was a Christian, but dared not see her. I was obliged to send someone to tell her about sister Huang.

Her cousin was not attacked during the Cultural Revolution because she worked in a hospital. With crowds of patients to keep everybody busy, people suffered less political pressure there. Besides, that cousin never bore witness for the Lord in her working unit. She dared not keep contact with sister Huang and so knew nothing about her mental condition. Now it was too late to do anything about it.

Besides praying for God's healing, I gave her cousin some money for food because I thought she needed more nutrition. Later, I thought it was no good for sister Huang to live alone. When I got her sister's address, I hurried to write and ask her to take sister Huang to Hangzhou for recuperation. I was really afraid that people from the police station would send her to a psychiatric hospital or farm because I had observed that there were several mentally disturbed people there.

Praise the Lord! Her sister came to Shanghai a day before I was returning to the labor camp and took her back to Hangzhou. The two sisters lived together and took care of each other. Sister Huang gradually got better and her mental disorder disappeared.

Sister Huang's mental sickness tells us how Satan tempts believers in every way not to rely on God. He urges us to solve our problems in our own ways, which will inevitably lead us to failure. Only those who rely on God will never be ashamed.

My treasures were safe

A few days before I returned to the labor camp, the general chief of our team issued a notice that the luggage of those who returned had to be checked. I arrived back on January 2, 1975. I was led to the office before returning to my living quarters. They called several team members to check everything I brought back with me. The cotton quilt bedding, clothes, daily commodities, food and medicine were all prepared by my two sisters, my niece and some brothers and sisters in Christ. The luggage was thoroughly searched.

Besides a letter, they did not find what they were searching for—a Bible. God already told me that they would search for my Bible. Therefore, I gave my concordance Bible to a sister in Christ. Did I not bring any Bible with me? Yes, I brought a copy of the book of Acts, a copy of Psalms and *The Secret of Power from on High* by Andrew Murray. I carefully hid them under the clothes I wore so the people who searched my luggage did not find them.

The letter they did find was written by a sister in Christ saying that she took some spiritual books from my room. At the end of the letter was a word of encouragement, "Love the Lord deeper." On the envelope, she only wrote my niece's name. I was very anxious about my niece and the sister. It was my niece who packed things for me. I did not have any idea how the letter got into my luggage.

In the camp, all my correspondence was checked, so I could not write to warn people about writing. However, the Lord who was doing wonderful things informed my niece just in time. The Psalmist says, "For he has not despised or disdained the suffering of the afflicted one. He has not hidden his face from him but has listened to his cry for help" (22:24).

When they finished searching my luggage, the chief ordered them to write on the blackboard everything I brought to the camp as a public abuse. The following evening I was called to the office by the reform chief. Being afraid that I could not see my way back in the darkness, I carried a flashlight with me and put it inside the pocket of my trousers.

When the chief saw my bulging pocket, she thought that I was going to bribe her, so she asked, "What is in your pocket?" I took out the flashlight. She had nothing to say. If I had wanted to give her something, I would be accused of bribery, and things would become very complicated.

Since she could find no fault with me, she only asked about the doctor who wrote the medical certificate for me, because the chief wrote on my permit of leave my sister's address in Putuo District. I said that I used to live in Hongkou District so I went to the hospital in that district. Later she asked, "Did you come back with someone else?" I said yes. My companion was visiting her relatives in Xuancheng. She knew that I told her the truth because I guessed that somebody had already reported it to her, and she knew that I was accompanied by someone on my way back to Anhui.

At last she was obliged to say, "Your leave was too long. Half of it shall be counted as overstaying of leave. There is no other reason than that you have a "cap" of being an anti-revolutionary." I felt that there was not use to argue with her. Let them count my leave however they wanted to.

I was content, happy and thankful that I had my rest of fifty days in Shanghai.

Every morning before we went out to work in the field, we listened to a lecture from the political instructor. I was criticized by the instructor during the morning gathering for bringing back too much luggage. Her purpose was to scare people into keeping a distance from me. However, those who wished to get something from me came to see me in secret.

To avoid offending those cadres, I started to attend indoctrination class the following day, January third. At the end of the month, I earned only one and half yuan for pocket money, less than those who did not attend labor at all, whose monthly pocket money was two yuan. It was unfair to give me so little pocket money since I was absent for only one day; and to count my leave as overstaying; and to take away the money that someone gave me. They did not even return the money through the post office. In the face of all these unfair treatments, I kept silent because I knew very well in Whom I believed.

One thing made me happy. My health was much improved. My Heavenly Father provided everything I needed. Was it necessary to be fussy about my unfair treatments?

Those who had a "cap" could not buy things except through the head of their group. They were persecuted, limited, bullied, despised, discussed, attacked, abused, criticized. I handed my burden to the Lord who gave me strength, and my inner self kept calm in all situations. But no one could stop me from praying or ask me to criticize my belief.

Seeing that I would not be reformed in the team, the general chief and political instructor decided to transfer me to another team. At noon on February 3 the instructor ordered me to move with other sick and aged team members to a dictatorship team on another farm. We left the next morning. Our luggage was sent by tractor. When we arrived there, I was placed in the dirtiest room. The shack above my bed, which was used to put traveling bags or cases, was loaded with big posters of *Mao's Quotations*.

On the first evening, I put a small toilet bucket at one end of my bed. The other end leaned against the wall. Early the next morning, our group leader did not allow me to use my own toilet bucket but ordered me to use the public one. One woman in our room had syphilis. All I could do was trust the Lord that I would not become infected.

We slept together on a big bamboo bed. Usually there were seven or eight people in one bed. The woman beside me had a mental disorder. The person next to her had been on leave for a long time, so she was used to enjoying more room. Now I was lying next to her, which made her very uncomfortable. She kept talking to herself until midnight.

God allowed these testings to try me like gold, to make me a vessel suitable for His use. When I thought it was God's hand testing me through those nonbelievers, I closed my mouth and committed myself to our righteous judge. Sometimes I prayed that God would stop the woman from talking at night. Praise the Lord, she did change!

On National Day, those who did not have a "cap" could have a kilo of peanuts. Those who had a "cap" had to work longer hours and enjoyed none of the benefits. One night the woman sleeping beside me put a handful of clean peanuts on my bedding. Suddenly she became my friend!

When I first came to that dictatorship team, the head of our group tried every way to make things difficult for me. Through my close communication with the Lord, I remained humble and gentle, and by His power treated everyone with love.

At first the chief of the team gave me only two and half yuan for pocket money. Later she proposed in our indoctrination class that my pocket money should be increased to three yuan. She said that I was working outdoors and needed to spend more money than those working indoors.

God's provision was sufficient! It is said in Luke 1:68: "Praise be to the Lord, the God of Israel, because He has come and had redeemed His people," and in Revelation 22:12: "Behold, I am coming soon! My reward is with me, and I will give to everyone according to what he has done!"

Chapter 13

On the Sick and Aged Team

Sketches of life

People on the sick and aged team were mostly over fifty, some even in their eighties. Except for a few with severe illnesses, we had to work very hard. Some who were assigned to raise pigs had to walk from the living quarters to the pig shed. When it was raining or snowing, it was hard walking on the muddy, slippery path. Other team members grew vegetables to supply the needs of the team. The best produce from the vegetable garden, such as watermelons, tomatoes and other vegetables, would be taken home by the general chief of the team in the shadow of night. The next best was taken by the other cadres, then by the staff members. The worst would be prepared for the sick and aged.

Every month the government would give each team member twelve yuan for food, but the chief in charge of our food supply was an inexperienced, irresponsible young offspring of high ranking officials. He bought pickles of very low quality at high prices, big bundles of rice noodles with grass wrapped inside, and firewood mixed with rocks with the money from *our* food budget.

Every day the cook had to make dessert for the chiefs who sat in the office chatting lightly and eating watermelon seeds, while the sick and aged struggled for breath under the scorching sun or in the frozen field. On holidays, the general chief would order the cook to make meat buns for the cadres to be taken home in the name of improving the meals of the team. Besides vegetables, they also grew staple food such as wheat, peanuts and oil vegetables. It was said that the sick and aged would be supported by the government. In fact, they themselves had to labor with blood and sweat to serve the cadres sent by the government. They labored even in rough weather and were despised and abused like slaves.

May was our busiest month. We had to go to the field at midnight and cut oil vegetables in the dim light of a flashlight. Sometimes in June we had to start cutting wheat before dawn. My job was to carry the collected wheat from the field to the barn to have it threshed and dried. That was heavy labor and nobody dared to take a break. When the chief on duty came later in the day, she inspected our work scornfully and criticized us, "You are a group of useless fools." However, I did not feel angry. On the contrary, I thanked our Sovereign God that He did not despise us nor forsake us, and that He even raised us to be ambassadors of the Kingdom of Heaven. What an honor it was! The world hated the Lord Jesus before it hated us Christians. However, our Lord is already raised to heaven and sits at the right hand of the Most High. At the thought of Him, my heart was filled with joy.

The Lord also comforted me with some special incidents to show me His care. One day while walking on the street, I saw my niece, Zhongchi, coming toward me with a traveling bag in hand. She was on her way from Shanghai to Shandong and took the chance to visit me. She stayed for seven days. Every day after I finished my work, we would sing hymns and pray, enjoying spiritual fellowship with each other. Zhongchi also brought me some nourishing food from Shanghai. Our diet was incredibly poor. Meat was rare and only served on festivals. The general chief would give the better part of meat to those who were in her favor, while someone regarded as her enemy only had something like the bone from the meat. Of course it was better than nothing.

Famine for chickens

Time passed quickly. In November, the general chief assigned me to raise chickens and to take care of more than a dozen cocks and hens. He was served eggs daily and chicken on festival days. I had to be careful that the chickens were not stolen and that they would not spoil the vegetable garden. The problem was that the chief did not give me any chicken feed. How should I feed them without any supplies? So I asked my Lord for food for my chickens. He provided all my needs. At that time the sick and aged could get some yams, besides rice or rice soup. Some team members were very kind to me. Early in the morning, they would send me their remaining food—rice soup and yams. A dumb person working in the canteen, when she washed rice beside the river, would give me a big handful of rice to feed the chickens. Sometimes, I would give her some candies, which made her happy.

The Lord taught me that unfailing faith draws me closer to Jesus, disperses all fears, paves the best path. Faith in the darkness is as in the brightness.

There was a hen which laid many eggs. She did not like rice soup. She walked beside me and pecked my hand with her beak, letting me know that she wanted some rice or chaff. So I would throw some rice in a hidden corner for her. When the chickens were hungry, they always came to me for food. Although small poultry, they understood to whom to go for food. What a pity that many people do not know that it is the Lord who gives them the breath of life. As it is written in Isaiah 1:2-3: "Hear, O heavens! Listen, O earth. For the Lord has spoken: I reared children and brought them up, but they have rebelled against me. The ox knows his master, the donkey his owner's manager, but Israel does not know, my people do not understand."

An interesting thing about a hen is that when about to lay an egg, she walks directly toward the coop. She is not distracted by anything on her way as if she is going on important business. Then a cock walks with her to the coop and waits until her egg is laid. Then he accompanies her back to their playground. There were about 100 meters between the playground and the coop, but they would make no detours to and from it. Chickens have such understanding, but the people of the world do not understand to worship and praise the Lord who gives them life. Lord, have mercy on us that we would have divine wisdom.

Supporting an anti-reformist

After raising chickens, I was assigned to guard the vegetable field which was frequently visited by peasants. Some of them came with bamboo baskets in hand and took away baskets of cucumbers, string beans, watermelons, or other vegetables. Others led cows to the field to eat soybeans there, so the chiefs arranged guards to look after the vegetable field day and night. Also, a field guard had to labor for two hours there, digging holes to plant vegetables, carrying buckets of water to irrigate the field, hoeing weeds, etc. I was assigned to field guard.

One day when I was weeding in the peanut field, I found several clusters of henna, in red, white, scarlet or pink. I dug them out and covered them with some weeds so they would not be dried under the sun. After I finished my duty, I took them back to the living quarters and planted them under the shade of the roof. For many years I had not planted anything. But this time, it was a success. I watered the flowers in the morning and evening, and the flowers bloomed with beauty. They even bore seeds. The Song of Songs 1:44 says, "My lover is to me a cluster of henna blossoms from the vineyard of En Gedi." It is said that where there is henna, there is no serpent. I pray that the Lord will help me to cherish Him in my heart and exalt Him above all so that Satan will find no foothold to attack me. James 4:7 says: "Submit yourselves, then, to the Lord. Resist the devil and he will flee from you." May the Lord turn His Word into my daily experience.

The year 1975 was ending and it was time for my annual review. An ordinary team member had only to make an annual report at the end of the year. Those who had a "cap" had to be reviewed by the masses and they would be abused and criticized over their speech and behavior according to other people's opinions or comments. All this was done in the good name of helping us improve.

There was a mentally disturbed prisoner on our team. One time I found her not going to work or eating for two days. I took the chance when there was nobody in the room to give her some biscuits. When she took the biscuits and ate them slowly, someone came in and saw it and soon reported it to the chief. Without asking me the facts, the chief criticized me in front of my group leader saying that I supported an anti-reformer who opposed the government and refused to reform her ideology, and that because I gave her biscuits, she refused to eat and work.

The incident was written on my annual review which had to be handed to the Labor Reform Bureau. I was not worried nor angry about it, but just handed the whole thing to the Lord. In the following year, a new leader came to our group. Without investigation, she repeated the story in my review form. The guilt of my giving away a few pieces of biscuits recorded in two of my annual reviews was unexpected. However, with the strength from my Lord, I did not argue with them. It was enough for me if the Lord knew it.

That winter, more people from Shanghai Prison were sent to our camp. One of them, who looked quite young, often hunched her back. When other people hurried to carry their luggage into the room, she still sat outside with her things scattered on the ground. Moved by the Word of God, "He will deliver the poor who are without help," I helped her move her luggage to the sleeping berth allocated to her. When she was sick, I secretly prepared two boiled eggs for her. Since my job was to guard the vegetable field, I had different working hours than the other team members, so I took some risks in telling her the Good News of Jesus Christ.

That young woman was often criticized in the political accusation meetings because she could not help complaining against the government. I prayed that the Lord would give me wisdom to help her. I knew that she would suffer more if I criticized her, which would certainly affect my gospel ministry. God answered my prayers so that almost every time when they held a political accusation meeting, I was on duty in the field. Occasionally, when I had to attend her accusation meetings, I would pray quietly for God's control over everything. He gave me wisdom so that I did not say any word to hurt her.

At my annual review, our group leader criticized me for sympathizing with an anti-reformer. To please the chiefs, some team members often bullied those who were labeled as anti-reformist, but I could not stand on their side against those poor people. I was criticized as losing the right stand and being in sympathy with anti-reformers. Then I would say, "That is what I am."

Opportunities for witness

Our general chief's husband was in charge of a male team. To elevate her husband's reputation, the general chief ordered us to cut grass to support the male team though we were all sick or aged patients. Each of us had to cut a certain quantity of grass in our spare time. A woman in our room had several husbands, like the Samaritan woman who met Jesus by the well. Now she had no husband at all. Some of her husbands forsook her; others were sent to labor camps. Her only daughter moved to Kaifeng in Henan Province when she got married. She was simple and frank, and worked hard. However, the director had a very bad impression of her because she did not know how to flatter the chief, sometimes even saying something foolish in front of the chief. She became easily irritated and often quarreled with other people.

On the morning of Chinese New Year, she was sewing a new quilted jacket and lost her spool of thread. She was very anxious because she wanted to finish the jacket so she could wear it on New Years, so I loaned her my sewing kit. She took out a spool of thread and said that the spool was hers. I felt sorry for her and went to look for the spool she lost, which was found in the sleeve of her jacket. Then she knew that she was wrong and was ashamed.

The Holy Spirit moved me to tell her the gospel when she was making shoes. It was inconvenient to speak too much in the living room so I took the chance when we were in the field. While cutting grass, I told her how the Lord Jesus came to deliver us sinners. She was converted and received Jesus as her Savior. I taught her how to pray, and I prayed that she would have enough strength to control herself from fighting with others. After we finished talking, we cut some more green grass to be carried back to the living quarters. When she saw that I had less grass than she did, she hurried to cut a big bunch of weeds and stuck it into my basket, thus to help me fulfill my quota.

It was unexpected that she would fight with a team member a week later. On that night, her mouth became twisted. After vomiting, she fell into a deep coma and died. I was so thankful that I took the chance to share the gospel, otherwise I would have suffered from bitter regret and blamed myself for not witnessing to her.

There was a woman with very poor eyesight in our team. People called her stubborn because she seldom admitted her faults and always insisted on having her own way. Since she never accepted other people's criticisms, no one liked to approach her.

She was a retired worker with a pension of over 80 yuan every month from the government labor insurance. During the Cultural Revolution, she was denounced as a landlady and abused and tortured in political accusation meetings. She felt life was meaningless and attempted to commit suicide by inhaling gas. Because the gas pipe did not fit well, a neighbor upstairs died of gas poisoning instead of her. The family of the dead person was so angry with her that they beat her cruelly and one of her eyes was blinded. Then she was arrested and all her possessions were confiscated. After she completed her sentence in prison, she was sent to our camp to receive labor reform. She also had the "cap" of class enemy and was often in deep distress.

When the general chief ordered us to cut grass, no one liked to go with her. I was enlightened that it would be a golden opportunity arranged by the Lord to preach the gospel to her, if I went with her. So I volunteered to cut grass with her and we both went to a distant area abundant with grass. There I told her all about the amazing grace of God. Praise the Lord, she confessed her sin and was willing to receive Jesus Christ to be her Savior. One day she fainted in the living quarters, but she was sound inwardly, and prayed that the Lord would save her. The Lord heard her prayer and she gradually came to herself again. Later her sister appealed for her and she was rehabilitated and went to live with her sister. Again she received a pension from the labor insurance every month, thus spending her late years at peace.

The full armor of God

Earlier, I mentioned that my mosquito net became the private, inner room for me to talk with the Lord. Every morning before dawn and every night after other people were asleep, I would kneel in the net to read the Word of God, and *The Secret of Obtaining Power from Above.* These were books I must read every morning. I must come to the Lord and listen to His voice before I meet any people.

At night, I would read the Psalms, being very careful not to be discovered. Otherwise, the book would be confiscated. Without the Word of God, I could not be nourished and fed spiritually, and I would not have enough strength to overcome all kinds of difficulties, oppression, abuse and attacks, and spiritual and physical weariness.

To meet my needs, I would open my heart to the Lord and read the Word of God with all my attention until I received a certain message from Him, whether it was a message of comfort, blame, guidance, or forgiveness. Limited by time, I did not read much, but I went deep into the Word of God. When I read, "But the needy will not always be forgotten, nor the hope of the afflicted ever perish" (Psalm 9:18), I became very happy as if the Lord was beside me to comfort me. I meditated on the verse and felt a joy overflowing in my heart which was greater than if I obtained an abundance of treasures or tasted many delicacies.

From the Book of Acts I read how Philip, Stephen, Paul and other disciples were filled and walked by the guidance of the Holy Spirit. I was enlightened and empowered by the message which gave me new hope and enabled me to follow the Lord willingly. I lived with patience, lowliness, love, joy and peace in all sufferings through trusting in the Lord. I was not afraid of being misunderstood, threatened, abused or falsely denounced because they served to push me to move forward and ascend to the higher mountain to enjoy a closer communion with the Lord.

The cold weather was a threat since I suffered from lung, heart and kidney problems and rheumatism. However, accompanied by my Lover, the Lord, I was courageous enough to run the difficult path with joy. One day we were building a bank in a distant place. There were two paths leading to the living quarters. One path was wider, but longer. The other was shorter, but it was a narrow and sloping mountain path with a rice field on the left and a deep ditch on the right. The weather was cold and the road was so slippery with ice that one could easily fall even on even ground, let alone a high mountain path. Still, I decided to take the short cut. Supported by my hoe I walked alone on that narrow path. I had to be extremely careful not to fall into the icy water in the ditch. I dared not look around or down, but kept my eyes straight forward while praying unceasingly in my heart. Step by step, I cautiously moved my weary feet toward the living quarters. Praise the Lord, He eventually led me to my destination.

Walking on the dangerous path on earth, we also have to take such precautions. Do we not have to be more cautious on the rough path of our pilgrimage? Must we not put on the full armor of God with the sword of the Holy Spirit in hand, the Word of God, and press toward the goal set by the Lord without looking at circumstances, nor ourselves, nor the power of Satan? Do I not have to rely more on the Lord, my Lover, keeping watch and continually uniting with Him, to avoid slipping into Satan's trap?

In the labor camp, Satan often stirred up people to disturb me spiritually. Sometimes when I took care of one person, another person would become jealous and she would make an exaggerated report to the director and abuse me. To make things even worse, they would write those things down in my annual assessment form as evidence of my crimes. Their purpose was to keep riding me. How should a Christian deal with these people? To be angry with them or to argue with them? No, the only way was to hand all these troubles to the Lord in prayer and tell Satan, "Let no one cause me trouble, for I bear the marks of Jesus" (Galatians 6:17).

Besides daily prayer, we sometimes have to pray in fasting against Satan to extinguish all the flaming arrows of the enemy. One of God's servants says, "The power of prayer comes from the perseverance of prayer," which is true. Every day when on duty, I would walk back and forth on the small lane between plots of the vegetable field and pray that the Lord, whom I served and to whom I belonged, would protect me to the end. I also prayed that the Lord would lead me to a higher rock. He answered my prayer.

Exempt from duty

Our financial chief was very arrogant. She was transferred to our team because some young people in the production team could not accept her. The aged people in our team usually obeyed her in everything. She flattered the higher-ups and bullied others. Once the authorities of the labor camp allotted our team a batch of raincoats, and each team member should get one. To please the authorities, the financial chief retained part of the raincoats and asked some people to buy their own from Shanghai.

The price of a raincoat was several yuan, which was about the same price of a pair of boots for outdoor labor. For many team members who did not receive anything from home, it was hardly possible to save that big sum of money for a raincoat. Many people were angry with her, but they dared not express their anger.

She often abused me and called me an element of the four groups of enemy. After liberation in Mainland China, four groups of people: landlords, rich farmers, anti-revolutionaries and bad elements in the society, were classified as class enemies by the Communist Party. When some people came to visit me, she would scold them, saying that they allied themselves with a class enemy. In December 1976, my eldest sister sent me a package which arrived on the evening of the 15th. Because I was classified as a class enemy, my package had to be opened in the office and examined by the financial chief.

When she found there were two cans of condensed milk in the package, she went into a rage. Knocking the table hard with one of the cans, she rebuked, "An element of four groups of enemies should not have such luxury." I never saw anyone so wild in my life. I managed to answer her calmly, "I did not ask for these foods. My sister sent the package to me of her own will." The chief continued to scold me, saying "If it happens next time, the package shall be returned." I replied calmly, "That is fine."

A day before the New Year of 1977, it was announced that those who had a "cap" should only work two hours on January 1, starting from nine in the morning. Since I had to be on duty in the afternoon, I did not have to work in the morning according to the regulation. As I went to the canteen for lunch and prepared to go to the shack in the field, I came across the financial chief. She was the chief on duty that day.

When she saw me going to the canteen with a rice bowl in hand, she thought it would be a good chance to retaliate. She asked, "What are you doing?" I said, "I am going to take my lunch and go on duty." She burst into foul words, "Element of four groups, why did you not work the two hours in the morning?" I said, "Because I have to be on duty in the afternoon." She became fierce and said, "Go and fetch a pair of bamboo baskets and a lifting pole." I had never carried a heavy load since I came to the camp. I had a medical report certifying that I suffered from heart trouble and should be exempted from heavy labor, but she insisted that I go and fetch these things. I obeyed her.

However, she was still not pleased. She continued to rebuke me and ordered me to follow her to the office. While shouting at me along the way, she pointed her finger at me until it almost touched my nose. She hoped that I would push away her hand and then she could accuse me of hitting her and organize a political accusation meeting to torture me. Praise the Lord that I was able to remain calm.

Before she finished her long-winded tirade, she accused me of still praying. Special grace and peace came to me from above which soothed away any inner disturbance, so I was able to stand firm to face all kinds of abuses. That day I experienced God's almighty power and great comfort. When it was time for me to be on duty, the labor group leaders came to the office and put a word in for me to the financial chief. They said, "She usually works very well and is never absent from duty." But the chief said, "There are so many of you. Why do you only want to have her on duty, not someone else?" Then she spat fiercely, "She shall not be on duty today."

Outside, flakes of white snow were dancing in the bitter north wind. Was it not better to sit in the warm living quarter to pray and do some private things, instead of enduring the weather on duty in the frozen field? At the thought of that wonderful arrangement, my heart was filled with thanks and praise. Psalm 76:10 says, "Surely your wrath against men brings you praise, and the survivors of your wrath are restrained." Were these words specially written for me? To the children of God, suffering is a blessing in disguise. Without the duty in the field, I could enjoy the two days off for the New Year like others.

Later someone came to visit me and thought I would be very angry to be abused by the financial director. Praise the Lord, with His company I had perfect peace and joy in my heart when eating my meal in the warm living room. After the meal, I began to work on my silk padded pants. I managed to fluff the silk stuff soft again in the two days off, which made the pants warmer and better fitting. Had the financial chief not abused me that day, I would not have had time to work on the pants.

Two days later, the general chief asked our group leader to tell me that she forgot about letting me rest for two days. Now I could go on duty. When I stepped outside the room, I found there was more than a foot of snow on the ground. It was very cold in the shack and I could hardly finish my meal before it was frozen with ice. Although I was cold bodily, I was very warm in heart. Looking at the beautiful white snow, I prayed that the blood of Jesus would cleanse my heart and make me whiter than snow.

Snow kept falling in abundance to form snow hills on the ground. With shovel or bamboo broom in hand, we tried hard to clear the path, but the path soon disappeared. When we were helpless with the snow, the sun slowly appeared from the clouded sky and mountains of snow gradually melted in the warmth of golden sunshine. I could hardly describe the excitement of seeing people walk safely up and down the mountain.

Many times the path of our pilgrimage is snowed over with difficulties so that we are obsessed with fatigue, sickness, poverty, and we are attacked, misunderstood and oppressed, making it seem like our way is blocked forever. We have made every attempt we can and cried for help. Still we see no hope. Take heart, the sun of justice will appear. As long as we live by faith and let everything be exposed to the rays of God's glory, every snow mountain will melt in due time. Therefore, we have no reason to fear.

I praised the Lord and asked Him for mercy upon those who were poor, sick, and aged and their deliverance from that financial chief. Three months later she asked for leave and went to Shanghai for medical treatment after being bitterly scolded several times by a mentally disordered patient. She never returned. Psalm 25:10 says: "All the ways of the Lord are loving and faithful for those who keep the demands of His covenant." I once again realized the supreme wisdom and abundant mercy of the Lord in whom I trust with all my heart.

Rest and praise

Earlier I mentioned a nurse who was imprisoned for writing some anonymous letters. After she completed her prison sentence, she was also sent to our team. She was very simple and easily irritated and often got into fights with others. One day, she bought a bottle of sliced orange in syrup for me, but how could she give it to me? If the chief found out about it, she would be criticized. So she put the bottle of sliced orange in the vegetable field and pointed out the spot in the distance to show me its place. However, it was discovered by a group leader with whom she often fought and was reported to the general chief. Consequently, she was criticized in a general assembly before the Spring Festival, saying that she took the same reactionary side with me.

The general chief's purpose was to warn all the team members to stay away from me and undermine the relationship between the nurse and me. Whenever God's blessings come to His children, Satan becomes restless. He will lure us to sin against God. If we patiently trust the Lord and rely on His strength, we will surely win.

In the labor camp, some made exaggerated reports about others to flatter the chief. It was common practice that they would stealthily break the team regulations once they gained her trust. Such people were most easily trusted. To protect themselves, the labor group leaders dared not report their faults.

The Spring Festival was drawing near. Those who had to be on duty in the field could not take a single day off during the festival, while I, being exempt from duty, could enjoy four days off in the Chinese New Year like other people. It was God caring for me in secret that I could have the four days holiday to prepare for my return to Shanghai.

George Muller said, "God handles everything that happens to me, and He controls the circumstances I am in."

After four days rest, the group leader asked me to go to work in the field carrying water, plowing the field and digging ditches. Praise the Lord, He gave me enough energy and strength to stand the hard labor. Later I was again assigned as a guard to take care of the tomato garden, a job that nobody was capable of. At first I was totally ignorant about how to grow tomatoes and the general chief was scornful of me in that she did not trust me to pick the tomatoes while they were young. However, I gradually learned how to take care of that vegetable through books and from experienced people.

Another reason that people did not like that job was that it wore out your clothes quickly. Because the paths between the rows of tomatoes were very narrow, your clothes were easily torn or stained. However, I preferred to work there because I could handle the job myself. I also could be alone with God and pray for other believers and ministers inside and even outside China. Sometimes, I sang hymns to praise the Ruler and Creator of the universe. Although I spent more time and money on that job, the spiritual benefits were beyond any material interests. Thus by managing the tomatoes, I not only gained earthly knowledge but also spiritual applications.

To be working in the tomato garden from early morning till late at night, some people suggested that the chief give me fifty cents extra pocket money. Thus, my monthly pocket money increased to three yuan and fifty cents.

The tomato's greatest enemy was an insect called the earth tiger. Hiding under the ground, it would break the main stem of a cluster of tomatoes so they could no longer bear fruit. Even if new sprouts might grow from the remains of the main stem, fruit would be delayed until much later. The earth tiger usually stayed in the soil close to the root, climbing up to the main stem in early dawn, then breaking the cane to suck juice from it. After it drank to its heart content, it hid in the ground again.

I learned from others to put some fresh grass in the lanes near the clusters of tomato and cover it with soil. Every morning, when I uncovered the soil, I found many earth tigers hidden in the grass and thus it foiled their work.

Besides catching earth tigers, I had to trim the clusters with scissors to cut off extra, quickly growing branches so that the remaining branches would yield bigger and better fruit. It reminded me that whenever the old life was predominant over the new life in my heart, I should deal with it without any delay. I should prevent sin from sprouting at all, such as irritation, anger, hypocrisy, selfishness, self-pity, self-righteousness, self-contentment, jealousy, and many other sins, walking by sight not by faith, etc. I should let the Holy Spirit cleanse anything the Lord deems unworthy, even what I do not consider bad, without considering my pain in the pruning. Then the Lord will become the center of my life and the glory of God will be manifested, I can bear much fruit to the glory of the Lord. (John 15:8)

James McConkey said that self-opinion is a strong fortress of the flesh and that to shatter it by surrendering to God's will is something most desired by the Holy Spirit. Unless we give up our every plan and totally yield ourself to the will of God, the Holy Spirit will not have complete freedom to work in us and we cannot bear much fruit. How precious are these words, like golden apples in silver settings.

At the end of 1977, when it was again time for the annual review, several group leaders joined our group to urge me to stop praying. They said that unless I stopped praying, I would never be able to have my "cap" taken off. They also mentioned that I had many relatives who would eventually draw away from me, if I remained a "capped" anti-revolutionary forever. However, the Lord gave me wisdom to see through this trick of Satan. By the power of God, I rejected the emotion of self-pity from the flesh and insisted firmly, "I cannot give up my prayer. It is my belief."

In one of the review meetings, the chief in charge of ideological education purposely said in our group, "Our country is still in need of translators. But it depends on what kind of books you are translating." She wanted me to criticize the book I translated with a promise of giving me a job as a translator in some research institute, but I told her right away, "My belief will never change." Immediately someone in the group retorted, "Then why don't you live on your religion? Why do you still depend on the government for food?" Quickly I responded to the question with a quote from a popular song, "The growth of everything depends on the sun." I asked, "Does the growth of everything depend on Chairman Mao?" They could not answer.

Later some who were concerned about me tried to persuade me to keep silent when I was criticized. They said, "You believe in Christ. Why do you have to tell it to other people? Isn't it better to keep silent and pray in your heart without outward posture? It will save you a lot of trouble. Now you tell others about your religion. It gives people a chance to attack and blaspheme the Lord. It is not wise." Among the people who tried to persuade me were Catholics, other Christians and non-believers. It seemed that their suggestions were logical and well-thought out. Actually it was a trick of Satan to get me to follow the flesh. I should never turn my ear to it.

In Ezekiel 33:3-4, the prophet says, "Their watchman sees the sword coming against the land and blows the trumpet to warn the people. If anyone hears the trumpet, but does not take the warning and the sword comes and takes his life, his blood will be on his own head." The Lord indicated to me that it would be the same as renouncing my faith, if I criticized the book that I translated. I must let other people know that I was firm about my faith and would never criticize it. My standpoint would never change, no matter how high the price. Otherwise, I would not be a follower of Jesus.

In my annual review meeting, the group leader told me, "Not to give up your religion means that you are not convinced you are guilty and therefore in defiance of the law. But the basic requirement to take off your "cap" is to admit your guilt."

That group leader often distorted my kindness to others as craftiness with ulterior motives. I had a big aluminum tub which was brought to the labor camp by a woman when she returned from her visit to her husband in Qinghai. She urged me to buy that tub because she needed money. And I did need a big tub because it was hard for me to pull the bed sheets out of the river after being wet in the water when we did our washing. So I bought the tub.

One day about six in the morning, a sick and aged woman in her seventies came to our living quarters to look for me. She wanted to borrow the big tub to wash her mosquito net and bed sheets. I was not there, and the group leader turned that poor woman down in my name. When she learned that I was on duty in the field, the old woman went up the mountain and found me in the shack. When I heard that she needed that tub, I hurried back to my living quarters. I pulled the tub out from under my bed and handed it to the woman. In the annual review meeting, the group leader used that story to accuse me of trying to draw that woman to my side.

There was another old woman on our team who had no connection with any relatives or friends. Because she drank tea and smoked, she had to spend much money every month. She had a flashlight which she used when she was on night duty. Later the director changed her job, and the flashlight became useless to her. I was on morning duty and had to get to the shack in the field at about five. In the winter on a rainy day it was still dark. Someone fell into a manure pit when walking in the dark. To avoid such a happening, I needed a flashlight. My old flashlight was out of batteries, and I could find nowhere to buy new batteries.

Since that old woman lacked money, she wanted me to buy both her flashlight and the batteries. I was sympathetic with her, so I bought her flashlight at the price she originally paid for the new one, though it had been used for quite a long time. When the group leader heard about it, she also used that story to verify that I was trying to bribe people.

There was a young woman sleeping beside me. She often took away the plastic bags that I placed on my suitcase and put them on her feet as rain boots on a rainy day. Some people who hated her criticized me, "That woman is not friendly to you. Why do you let her take away your plastic bags?" I answered casually, "She stole them. I did not give them to her." In the annual review meeting, the same group leader challenged me over that issue, "Why do you not criticize her of her theft in her review? It proves you are telling a lie." However, I did not want something bad added to her annual review over such a small thing which might affect the decision to take off her "cap."

In the end, the director asked me, "Are others criticisms against you true to the facts?" I answered, "Some are true, others not. But there is no need to justify myself." For the sake of the Lord, I did not care what kind of "cap" was being put on me nor did I suffer from it. My heart was very calm and full of praise. I firmly believed that God would settle everything in due time. As long as I could please the Lord that was good enough for me. No matter how I was criticized of "bribery," "instability in political views," "lying," etc., I should be patient in the Lord and trust Him.

One day, I talked a little with sister Q when she was going to the toilet room. The group leader saw it and reported it to the chief. Therefore the chief criticized me, "It is an anti-revolutionary activity." I said nothing and just kept silent. Every day I would use the time on duty to pray for many things. That was a blessing.

One day in midsummer, a load of pears was distributed to our team and each team member who attended labor could have two and half kilos of them. The dozen people in our living quarters received several dozen kilos. The group leader did not want to divide the fruit, so she asked someone else to do it. That person was very selfish. She chose the good pears for herself and those who were friendly to her, leaving bad ones for the three mentally disturbed roommates. That day I was a substitute for the group note taker who was transferred to another team, and since I had the right to say something over the issue, I suggested using a scale and dividing the pears according to weight without separating the big from the small ones.

One of the mentally disturbed patients, named Chou, was still young. She was imprisoned because of doing speculation business. She was denounced by her husband who was released while she was sent to prison. The poor woman missed her family day and night. She even managed to dry some yams, allotted to her as winter food, that she could carry back home. She saved her pocket money each month and put aside the yearly subsidy for clothes. One day her dream came true and she was allowed to go home, but her children did not welcome her to stay at home for long because of her mental disease.

After using all her savings, her children cheated her by saying that they would send her to a doctor, but actually they sent her back to the labor camp. How could I follow others to wrong such a poor parent? How could I do injustice and pursue personal gain in the group? No, a servant of God could never do such a thing!

I went to borrow a scale and divided the pears equally for each one. Then I placed the pears at the front of each person's bed. When I carried the pears to the bed of a mentally disturbed patient and placed them in her tub, she was annoyed. She thought it was not hygienic to put the pears in the tub which she used to wash her feet. To retaliate, she poured a tub of dirty water into my tub, saying, "You have not been reformed yet since your stay in the city prison and you still pray before meals." Someone reported the incident to the chief.

One afternoon when I was going to take a nap, the group leader came to ask me to go to the general chief's office. As soon as she saw me, the chief said, "According to the regulation of the farm, one cannot speak or behave willfully. Do you know that?" I replied, "I did not speak wildly nor behave willfully." The group leader was standing outside the office and thought I would be fiercely criticized. However, it was an opportunity that God prepared for me to witness the truth before the director.

The chief said, "Don't say grace with the bowl of rice in hand." I said, "It is OK not to take hold of the bowl, but it is impossible not to say grace for my meal." That afternoon, God gave me special courage to testify to the truth. She then said, "Christianity is a tool used by Imperialists to invade our country." I told her that the gospel was spread all over the world from a very small country by the Mediterranean Sea called Judah. Many missionaries who came to preach the gospel in China were volunteers. They were strongly opposed by their own relatives and friends. I added, "If it is not empowered by God, I would have died or, at the very least, became mentally disturbed."

Later she said, "Do you know that others say that you are very stubborn?" I said calmly, "I don't mind however they criticize me." I also witnessed to her how I was moved by the Lord before I was arrested and how things happened as God indicated. Then I told her the testimonies of many great scientists. The group leader remained outside the window, eavesdropping.

When I returned to our room, the people there were surprised to see me beaming with a smile. I was able to keep calm and firm and deal with my enemy in a just attitude because I kept talking with the Lord every morning. It was God who protected me with shields of His amazing grace.

There was a mentally disturbed patient named, Tang Quiying. The chief asked me to take care of her finances and needs. One day she went alone to the other side of the vegetable field after we finished the day's labor. It was nearly dark when I returned and all the people were eating supper. When I did not see Tang among the group, I asked, "Where is Tang?" People told me that she did not return. I hurried to the canteen to get some food and went out to look for her. Actually the group leader should take the responsibility to find her, but she asked me to do it, so I went out alone.

After searching for quite a while, I found her straw hat and a pair of baskets with the carrying pole laid beside the vegetable field. But where was Tang? The sun was descending in the west, birds returned to their nests and the sky was wrapped by dark clouds. I became very anxious because with my poor eyesight it would become harder for me to detect the hiding place of Tang under the dark shade of ascending night. I decided to report it to the chief and ask for help.

I returned to the living quarters and found only the business chief in the office. She ordered all the people in our room to go searching for her. Then the group leader was obliged to go with us. I went out again with another aged woman, this time wish a flashlight in hand. Tang was finally found and taken back home.

In a meeting after the incident, the group leader gave all the credit to herself. Then she asked if I had anything to say. I shook my head. I thought it was meaningless to compete for credit. It is all right if the Lord knows it.

Chapter 14

New Assignments and Trials

Plowing

In the beginning of August 1977, the two groups of sick and aged, still regarded as enemies, received a new task. We were to help the male team pull sprouts of rice. The muddy water in the rice field was hot under the scorching sun. Sweat streamed down our bodies and mixed with the muddy water. The soil was deep and sticky. It was hard for me to move my feeble legs in the sticky soil and a real challenge for me not only to move but to pull up a certain quantity of sprouts to complete the quota. Should I refuse to go? No, I could not. As long as possible I tried not to ask the general chief for anything.

One day, when I followed another team member on duty, I found some crops were stolen from the field of which I was in charge. I immediately went to report it to the general chief. Otherwise, she would think that all things were stolen on my duty. As I reported it to her, she turned her back to me and said, "You bore me to death." If I begged her for mercy to be exempted from the labor of pulling rice sprouts, I could not glorify the Lord. Paul says, "I can do everything through Him who gives me strength." I prayed with all my heart for strength that I could do something beyond my capacity through Him.

With a stick in hand, I could move better in the sticky soil. The Lord sent a very experienced team member to work with me. With her guidance and help, we did not lag behind. When working in the rice field, I tucked the ends of my pants into my socks and bound them tightly with strings; thus, the leeches could not cling to my legs.

There was a person whom the general chief liked very much because she kept on telling her about other people's faults. She also carefully bound her legs, but only a few minutes after she stepped into the muddy water the leeches kept clinging onto her legs, which not only affected her health but interfered with her work. However, the merciful God was taking care of me in everything, and He helped me to keep up with other members in that hard labor. Psalm 10:14 says: "The victim commits himself to you, you are the helper of the fatherless."

Satan still took every chance to attack me. One day, I was digging holes with two other people in the vegetable garden. One of them made the holes too big. The chief came and criticized us fiercely. Assuming that the holes were made by me, she shouted, "Who made these holes? They are too big." I was muddled at her shouting and forgot who made these big holes so I said nothing. Then the group leader added, "You can only do well when you are watched from behind." At that moment, the Lord gave me special memory and courage, and I answered them bravely, "It is true that one shall not remember the bitterness of hard experience and write down what she did." Then I told them which lanes of holes were made by whom in detail. The chief and the group leader closed their mouths.

One afternoon, I went plowing for two hours with a dozen of other people. Two in the group plowed too shallow. When the chief asked who did that, a person who gave up her belief put the blame on me. However, a labor group leader stood up and proved that it was not me. She said that I had only been there for two hours. After I left, she continued the lane I started so she knew very well which lane was done by me. The Lord, my Father, protected me. The chief and the person who made the false report were obliged to give up. Many a time the Holy Spirit would reveal to me the words that I said or something that I totally forgot to bring shame to the enemy. "Lord, no one whose hope is in you will ever be put to shame. But they will be put to shame who are treacherous without excuse" Psalm (25:3).

Hardship reveals our inner selves

The weather in Maple Ridge, Anhui Province, was very changeable. It was cold in the morning and evening, hot and suffocating at noon, and windy and stormy in the afternoon. During a storm, some big trees were blown down, while others whose roots grew deep not only stood firm, but stretched their roots even deeper. It reminded me that God often uses hardship to reveal to us the inner status of our lives.

On September 11, 1977, there suddenly came a great storm in the afternoon. The wind was swirling and rain was pouring down. There was thunder and lightning, making a horrible sight in the sky. I was alone on duty in the shack. Rain was pouring into my shelter and I was wet through. The poles of the shack were tilted one by one toward the east making a cracking noise, signaling that the shack might collapse. I was afraid that my pots and bowls would be ruined if it fell. So I carried my things in a basket to the living quarters. With water streaming down the muddy mountain path it was very difficult to walk, but I had to hurry back on duty because thieves knew that people on duty usually would go back to the living quarters in such a storm. They would take that opportunity to come and plunder the field.

When I returned, the wind swept over the field with new momentum. It blew down the electric poles and tore apart the wires. The poles of the shack were almost blown off balance. I thought if the wind blew down the shack, the people on night duty would have no shelter for the night, and if it fell while they were sleeping, they would be hurt.

I remembered that we had a carpenter in the living quarters. It would be much better to ask him to add two strong poles on the east side of the shack to prevent it from falling. Although old and weak, I decided to try my best by the Lord so I went down the mountain and found our chief who was on duty that day. I told her about the shack and asked if she could send the carpenter to reinforce it. In response, she gave me a good lecture, "You are poisoned by capitalist ideology. Why can't you overcome such a small difficulty? You see the people on the opposite mountain have no shack. Still, they stay on duty." Actually, the people on the opposite mountain had already returned to their rooms.

What should I do in the face of such rudeness? Should I be angry with her or bear hatred against her or groan with vehemence or grieve with despair or mourn or complain or languish or take the attitude of escapism? No, with the Lord for company, I should do nothing but find peace and joy in Jesus. It is written in Job 34:29, "If he remains silent, who can condemn Him?" With good patience, I said, "The shack may stand the wind for a while, but the people on night duty will be in danger if it falls in the dark. Would you please tell them to be careful?" As I returned to the mountain, I saw the shack had already blown down, together with some trees.

If I would have been there, I would have been injured or scared. However, the Lord who was looking after me with His meticulous care protected me once again. Nothing, neither the roaring storm nor severe criticism, could take away the divine peace in my heart.

While on duty, the most exciting thing for me was to see the morning stars twinkling in the dark sky before dawn. I could not help singing with joy, "He is the lily of the valley and the bright and morning star. He is the fairest of ten thousand to my soul." Sick and weak, I was like a bruised reed and a smoldering wick. However, the Sovereign God opened my eyes and let me see the morning star, rekindling my hope that darkness, which seemed to be endless, will pass away and morning will eventually come.

In the farm, whether it was sunny or rainy, there were always thieves looking for a chance to rob our crops. If they were caught, the person on duty could not call them thieves; otherwise they would beat up the person and demand a letter of apology. Therefore, I had to rely on the strength and wisdom from God to deal with them.

One time, the chief assigned a crippled team member to be on duty in the vegetable field. That woman was bad tempered and behaved like a gangster. She was very fierce toward the peasants who attempted to steal our crops and cursed them in foul words. The peasants retaliated by throwing stones at her head. More crops were stolen when she was on duty than at other times. When I saw peasants leading a cow to our field, I would talk with them gently, "Be kind to us. We are all sick and aged. It is not easy for us to grow vegetables. Would you please not let the cow eat our plants?" Then the peasants would go away.

Besides dealing with the greedy peasants, I also learned to take care of the crops. Red beans and green beans ripened in the deep autumn. When ripe beans fell on the ground, I would pick them up. The shell of the red bean was earth brown, but the bean inside was very pretty. Those still on the cluster were light red and bright red; those fallen on the ground were dark red. The shell of the green bean was dark brown or black, while the beans inside were grass green. I was fascinated by the marvelous creation of the Almighty God.

Praise the Lord who sends the Holy Spirit into my heart, I am able to persevere in all circumstances and to become strong and stand firm, and overcome the flesh, the world, and Satan with his evil power. The power of the Holy Spirit fosters growth in our spiritual life. It is like having the treasure in jars of clay, "to show that this all-surpassing power is from God and not from us. We are hard pressed on every side, but not crushed; perplexed, but not in despair, persecuted, but not abandoned; struck down, but not destroyed. We always carry around in our body the death of Jesus, so that the life of Jesus may also be revealed in our body" (2 Corinthians 4:7-10).

Man cannot conquer heaven

There is a Chinese saying, "Plans are made by man, but they are accomplished by Heaven." That was absolutely true on the farm. Every year our team would hold a resolution announcement assembly right before we started spring and summer sowing in order to mobilize everyone to work hard. The year 1978 was as usual. A high sounding slogan for that year was "Man must win over Heaven," which was shouted by several team spokesmen. I was very worried about it. It was all right that everyone took responsibility to work his best. However, it was presumptuous and boasting against God to announce that one was superior to heaven. How dangerous it was!

"To fight against Heaven" was even added to the camp regulation, a new rule to be observed by all. We were ordered to memorize the camp rule: "Man must win over Heaven." I changed the word "Heaven" to "weather." People who did not believe in God said that I avoided the word "Heaven" because of my religion. I remained firm in my faith and never changed my point of view.

That summer was particularly hot with severe drought. Streams were dried up, wells became muddy dens and all spring water disappeared. We had to wash our clothes in a river far away from the living quarters. To insure the supply of drinking water, we stopped irrigating fields. Vegetables and rice withered and many rice fields turned into huge, dry, turtle shells. The production of rice drastically decreased. The slogan and the resolution announced in the assembly became as disappearing bubbles. It is dangerous to boast to man, but it is more dangerous to boast to Heaven, let alone to boast against Almighty God who created heaven and earth. Proverbs 27:1 says: "Do not boast about tomorrow, for you do not know what a day may bring forth."

To make things worse, bad news reached the team. There was an earthquake in Liyang, a neighboring district, where some people were injured and killed. Our camp was within the area affected by the earthquake. Therefore everybody, including cadres, staff members, and their families had to sleep outdoors. Men and women were all in a panic, some in tears. At midnight, people from the living quarters were all sitting in the vegetable field. However, those who trusted the Lord were not anxious or frightened. We knew that the Lord had established His throne in heaven, and His kingdom rules over all. Without His permission, not a hair of our heads will fall.

While people escaped to the field at midnight, another Christian and I took the opportunity to have close communication with the Lord in peace. We had peace in our heart because we knew "in whom we believe," and that the earthquake fulfilled Bible prophecy that the day of Jesus' coming was near and we should be ready to meet Him in His glory. The catastrophes—storm, drought and earthquake—which came in succession distinguished God's children from worldly men and served as a warning to those foolish men who thought that they could win over Heaven by their own strength.

Satan's tricks

One day, the general chief asked all the team members to hand in their shoes. At first we were puzzled. Later we learned that a robbery had taken place in the headquarters and our shoes were checked to see if they matched the footprints at the scene of the crime. The story went like this:

> The accountant of the headquarters had a good friend. He often came to play with the keys to the safe used by the accountant. One day, when the accountant was sound asleep, his friend opened the safe and stole more than 10,000 yuan. This was equivalent to all the wages for people working in several teams as well as many nationwide circulated food coupons. When he learned the secret of opening the safe, he took the opportunity to steal all the valuable things.

Does not our enemy Satan play the same trick? Sometimes, he looks like a roaring lion ready to devour God's people. As such, he is easily recognized. However, he sometimes works in the disguise of an angel of light. When we are lonely, in poverty, hungry, grieving, fatigued, sick, or failing in our business, he will even work through the caring of our relatives, coworkers or neighbors and tempt us to leave the narrow path and give up our commitment to the Lord. If we are not watchful, we will accept his temptation and fall into his trap, thus losing the treasure from God. Therefore we must be alert lest we lose our treasure before we know it.

Our Heavenly Father has already given us the keys to the kingdom of heaven. He says, "I will give you the keys of the kingdom of heaven. Whatever you bind on earth will be bound in heaven, and whatever you loose on earth will be loosed in heaven" (Matthew 16:19). By His strength may we understand how to use the keys properly. Let us avoid spending precious time satisfying the cravings of sinful man, the lust of our eyes. If we do not bind Satan and resist evil, we give footholds to the world, the flesh and the devil. What a loss!

Usually, we spend much time eating, dressing or casually talking and judging others. Unconsciously, we lose our spiritual power. How grievous it is that we are robbed without being aware of it. Satan's favorite trick is to rob Christians of their prayer time.

One Sunday morning, I lifted up my eyes to the Lord when a team member came into the dirty shack. She sat in front of me and began to talk about this and that person. I felt uncomfortable because Satan was robbing my precious time with the Lord. So I told her that according to the regulation of the farm people who were not on duty, they were not allowed to stay in the shack except on rainy days. Consequently, she left. Immediately I returned to the throne of grace to continue my close communication with the Lord.

Isaiah 59:16 says, "He [The Lord] saw that there was no one, He was appalled that there was no one to intervene; so His own arm worked salvation for Him." Let us be cautious and self-controlled, praying that the Lord helps us to seize the opportunity and bind Satan with powerful prayer, to loose slaves of sin, and protect us from being like that foolish accountant who lost the key to the safe.

Rainbow after the rain

In my gloomy surroundings, God still cheered me with some light. Several times during the rain, I saw a beautiful rainbow in the sky. I was encouraged that the Lord who made the covenant with Noah was the same Lord who made a covenant with me. The Lord "will not always accuse, nor will He harbor His anger forever" (Psalm 103:9). He heals what He tears and wraps what He wounds.

When I was downcast spiritually, the Lord prepared a prayer partner for me. She was several years younger and often came to pray with me for the church and also for ourselves. She often prayed for my return home. In 1977 I applied for a home visit, but my application was turned down. But through our prayer with one heart, the Lord let me know that I would get permission for a leave soon.

Actually, I got my permission and left the farm on March 15, 1978. Before dawn I, together with other team members who were also going to Shanghai, took a bus to Guangde, Anhui, nearby where John and Betty Stam, a young missionary couple of the *China Inland Mission* were beheaded as martyrs in 1934. They left their nursing baby who was secretly cared for and fed by a peasant sister in Christ and was later sent to relatives. In Guangde, I changed buses to Shanghai.

The small room where I lived before I was arrested was occupied by my grandnephew and the nanny who looked after him. Because they did not expect my return, I slept on the floor the first night. The following day, an old neighbor of the nanny who was a Christian came to visit her. It had been a long time since her last visit, and she was very happy to meet me. When she learned that I would be able to stay home for a while, she insisted that my grand-nephew and the nanny move to her home. I could then sleep in my own bed and have a quiet place to keep close communion with God. Had God not sent that believer to visit the nanny just then, I would not have had peace at home during my half a month leave.

The Christian neighbor also loaned me her copy of *Streams in the Desert* and the Bible. The message for March 15 in *Streams in the Desert* was:

> "Do not be afraid, O worm Jacob, O little Israel, for I myself will help you," declares the Lord, your Redeemer, the Holy One of Israel. "See, I will make you into a threshing sledge, new and sharp, with many teeth. You will thresh the mountains and crush them, and reduce the hills to chaff" (Isaiah 41:14-15).

March 29 was the date for me to return to the labor camp. When I got up around three for my morning devotions, I read the same verse in the Bible. He showed me His mercy because two days before I had found with great joy a pocket New Testament in the small attic. God preserved that precious book for me so that I could continue to read His Word after returning to the camp. He must still have a plan for me!

It was not easy for one to be released permanently. Many team members who had children were unable to leave and join their families, let alone a single woman like me. But I knew for certain that there is nothing impossible to the Lord. He is able to do everything. A servant of God wrote, "God asks us to pray for something impossible. God can achieve what man is unable to. Otherwise, He is not God."

The Lord of wonderful deeds will do what we are unable to. He also enables us do what others cannot, as long as we rely on Him. We are able to do what is impossible to man when we see the invisible God through our spiritual eye. Inspired by the Word of God and moved by the Holy Spirit, I began to be aware of small patches of clouds as were seen by the servant of Elijah. And I knew that the time drew near when I would finish my hard life in the labor camp and leave there to serve elsewhere the Lord who reigns overall.

Chapter 15

Truth Will Win

My appeal made

It was the winter of 1978. Chairman Mao, who had been looked upon by so many as almost a god, had died like all mortal men. China was poised for great changes and much turmoil and uncertainty. We, who were still in labor camp, could not speculate what would happen next, nor how it would affect us.

An old woman who had a "cap" of landlady came to me one day very confused and told me in secret that she saw a big poster at the team office on which the names of Jiang Qing, Zhang Chunqiao, Yao Wenyuan and Wang Hongwen were crossed out. The four formed a political clique called the "Gang of Four" which earlier had helped Mao Zedong in his attempt to wipe out his political enemies. But they attempted to take over as rulers of the country after the death of Mao. She asked me what it meant. By the end of the year, the whole truth came out.

Throughout history, ruthless tyrants all over the world have ruled only temporarily. When the day of their doom came, they fell and perished. The fate of the "Gang of Four" was the same. However, the Word of God will last forever.

For several nights in November 1978, I was awakened at midnight and could not fall asleep again, which was unusual. I always slept very well and was never troubled with insomnia. Why could I not sleep during these nights? God wanted to open my ears and reveal His will unto me. Under the quilt by flashlight I read the Bible, chapter after chapter. One day I read that Jesus ordered the people around the tomb to roll away the grave stone before He called Lazarus to come out. The Lord reminded me that one shall do one's duty, but I did not know what I should be doing.

On December 15, a sister in Christ came from the production team to our sick and aged team telling me that Jiang Hua, the Judge of Supreme People's Court in Beijing, made a speech of "Seeking Truth from Fact." In the speech, Jiang Hua said that cases should be judged according to the facts, not be magnified, thus pronouncing somebody anti-revolutionary because he said something inappropriate under certain circumstances. Some young people in my former production team were discussing my case saying that I should make an appeal to the court.

Then a rehabilitated overseas Chinese who had no prior contact with me came to see her friend in our team. When she saw me she said, "You should appeal to the court for a reversal of the verdict. At least, they will let you go home."

Later I read that speech by Jiang Hua, the Judge of Supreme People's Court, and found that what I had heard was true. Still I waited patiently before God and dared not to write anything yet to see how He would fulfill His will.

By the end of December, I thought that I should visit the production team and see if there were any changes in the situation. With the "cap" of anti-revolutionary, I was not allowed to move around. Then God let me read the story of Apostle Paul appealing to Caesar in Acts 25:11.

In my former production team, there was a team member who was very friendly to me. When her husband came from Shanghai to visit her, my sister asked him to bring me a parcel. When the chief called me to pick up the parcel from her office, I asked permission to go to the production team to ask the visitor to take something back to Shanghai for me. My request was granted.

When I arrived there, I saw the woman who had consulted me about her divorce. At the sight of me, she said, "Write your letter of appeal promptly. I will read it and make any necessary corrections for you." Still I was hesitant. Then I visited another friend in the team. In her room, I met the young girl who liked to make jokes at me. As soon as she saw me, she said, "Jesus, Jesus, I thought you had gone home a long time ago. Why do you still stay on the farm? Write a letter of appeal! Quick!" Being urged by several people, I began to understand that the verse of taking away the stone from the tomb of Lazarus, which I read in November, instructed me to write an appeal.

Afraid that my writing would be interrupted if I were discovered, I hid in the duty shack to write my letter of appeal. I then asked someone to forward it to the woman who promised to make corrections for me. The woman, having gone through my letter of appeal, told me that I should write it in a certain format and emphasize the important evidence against my verdict. So I rewrote the appeal and prepared it in three copies.

On the morning of January 13, 1979, I asked permission to go and send my letter of appeal. The chief thought that I did not need to appeal, saying that my case would be reversed. I said, "I need to clarify some points." With God's help, I staggered over the snow-covered field to a post office more than two miles away and sent the letter of appeal to the Shanghai Supreme Court and the Hongkou District Court.

In the letter of appeal, I mentioned that the book I translated and the article of my reflection were purely concerned about the spiritual life of a Christian and had nothing to do with politics and contained nothing harmful. As for praying "do not let Satan work among the leaders of the country," it was a Christian prayer to God, not a curse. I also supported my arguments with some facts to verify that my verdict of committing anti-revolutionary crime was not based on facts.

In the early morning of January 29, 1979, the second day of the Lunar New Year, the chief in charge of our ideological reform came to our team and told us that there were three requirements to be considered for taking off one's "cap": first, to be enthusiastic in labor; second, to observe regulations and laws; and third, not to do bad things. The declaration of such good news and a speech made by the Minister of *Public Security Department* in the same tone instilled hope into the hearts of those of us who were still wearing a "cap" and brought smiles to our faces.

I gave away things that I was not planning to take home and waited every day for the announcement to have my "cap" taken off. The stars at dawn foretold the appearing sun of God's blessing. My niece in Shandong was anxious because she feared that I could not stand the bitter life in the labor camp so she invited me to live with her. Being afraid that she might be involved in my case, as I still had a "cap," I declined her invitation.

Some brothers and sisters in Christ also were concerned and hoped that I would ask for a leave of absence to Shanghai. However, I felt that I must wait until my "cap" was taken off and it was declared by the government that I was no longer an anti-revolutionary. God saw that I still had to learn to be patient, and He wanted me to wait in faith until the time of His rescue. When His time came, the impossible would become possible.

On February 2, 1979, I received a letter from *Shanghai Supreme Court* informing me that my case was transferred to the *Hongkou District Court.* In mid-March, the Hongkou District Court sent me a letter through my eldest sister saying that because of a backlog of such cases they needed time to review my case, and that they would contact me as soon as possible. Then I got a message from God, "Be patient, then, brothers, until the Lord's coming. See how the farmer waits for the land to yield its valuable crop and how patient he is for the autumn and spring rains. You too, be patient and stand firm, because the Lord's coming is near" (James 5:7-8).

Off with "the cap!"

The discipline of waiting provides a good chance for us to practice our faith as it demands exclusive reliance on God to wait for His time and delivery. Waiting is not easy. As time passes by, we become too anxious to wait for God's deliverance and impatiently employ our own methods. This is as foolish as people getting impatient waiting for the butterfly to come out of its cocoon and trying to pull it out prematurely by hand. Through waiting, God enlightens us and helps us to root out of its cocoon our hidden faults. To wait for the Lord shows our respect for Him, and we are refreshed with strength from above. As I realized the importance of waiting, I became very calm.

One morning when I was talking with the Lord, I received a message from the Gospel of Matthew: "The people living in the darkness have seen a great light; on those living in the land of the shadow of death a light has dawned" (4:16), and I became more aware that the day was near.

In the afternoon meeting of June 8, the list of those whose "caps" were taken off was pronounced. *My name was included on the list!* The word that the Lord had given to me was: "Call to me and I will answer you and tell you great and unsearchable things you do not know" (Jeremiah 33:3).

My faith was strengthened after my "cap" was taken off. I asked someone to carry two pieces of my luggage to the post office and have them sent to Shanghai. Then I moved with all those whose "caps" were taken off to the living quarters for farm workers. There I lived with many strangers in one room knowing nothing about their nature. Since it was God's arrangement for me, I accepted it in faith and waited patiently for His time.

Soon I received a letter from my eldest sister informing me that someone from the Labor Reform Bureau had visited her to discuss my return home. Eventually faith had turned into reality! God's promise was fulfilled. On July 24, I received from the team treasurer some money as a subsidy and completed all the procedures for leaving.

The next morning, I got on a bus bound for Shanghai with another person who had also appealed to the court. A chief and a team member helped us put our luggage on top of the bus and stood by the bus to see us off. I invited them to visit me if they ever came to Shanghai. Hardly had I finished my words when an unfamiliar woman snapped sharply, "To Shanghai and listen to your sermon in your church? You should thank so and so; otherwise, you would still be on the farm." I was at a loss for a reply as I was never eloquent nor quick in responding. So I prayed that God would give me the wisdom and power to respond to her challenge.

I was then struck by the Word of God, "Truth will win," which I repeated two times. Praise the Lord! The woman closed her mouth. For the sake of the Lord, I still chatted with her kindly, asking where she came from and where was she going. Then I learned that she was a visitor.

During lunch time, passengers got off the bus to buy food in the canteen. Seeing that the woman did not have a food coupon, I gave her a coupon distributed countrywide for half a kilo of food. Although she returned the coupon to me after she found out that the canteen of the bus station did not charge food coupons, she became very friendly to me. Glory be to the gracious Lord!

The one who left the camp with me used to be the head of a labor group so she had known the date for our departure ahead of time and had written to ask her family to pick her up at the bus station. When we arrived, they were there waiting for her. They put her luggage on a small truck and drove away.

I did not know the date of my release until two days before leaving, and then it was too late to inform my sister about my arrival. Now I was left alone by the roadside with my luggage. I prayed that God would provide a car for me. People told me that I could call a taxi from the bus station across the street, but how could I cross the street with so much luggage? I prayed for help.

Then I saw an old man with a woman and a child standing beside a small truck. I asked them to drive me home. They refused because they were not in that business. They had come to the bus station to pick up the child. The young woman was very kind and she suggested that the old man give me a ride to the bus station so that I could find a taxi for hire. While I went into the bus station to find a taxi, the old man stood outside to watch over my luggage. As my house was far away, the taxi driver was reluctant to go so I asked to be driven to my sister's place.

On July 25, 1979, about four in the afternoon, I arrived at my sister's home! Because the *Labor Reform Bureau* had contacted the *Public Security Bureau*, I soon had my permanent residency registered and my ration coupons for oil and food secured. In due time, God's time, the heavily locked iron gate had opened by itself. Oh, my Lord shepherded me with integrity of heart, with skillful hands He led me.

Mr. C. E. Yu, a son of God's servant who translated *The Practice of the Presence of God* by Brother Lawrence and *Sweet Smelling Myrrh*, an autobiography of Madame Guyon, had sent me a letter saying that he wanted to be the first to welcome me and bring something that I would cherish most—the Bible. Things happened as he wrote in the letter, which impressed me so much. Mr. Yu was so kind that he not only came to see me, he offered to help me if there was anything to be done that required physical labor.

Brother Yu was forced to be separated from his wife and children when he was still young and suffered in the labor camp for many years for the sake of the Lord. Eventually, he was delivered by the mighty hand of the Lord. I did not know him, but he had learned my story from one of his fellow prisoners. The spiritual battle had lasted for so many years. But God's truth had won in the end, and His children came back home to worship in awe and homage their Savior, the Almighty and Everlasting God.

Living at home

When I returned home, I learned that one of my former students from the orphanage came from Shandong twice to look for me. He was only about three or four years old when he was in our orphanage, a very lively and lovely boy. We called him "Little Baby." When our orphanage merged with Bethany, he went along with the other children. Later Bethany was moved to Gansu by the Civil Bureau. The boy escaped from the orphanage several times.

Now, twenty-seven years later, he had grown into a fine young man. When he came to my house and saw the nanny who was there to look after my sister's grandson, he said, "I cannot help myself from shedding tears when I approach the gate of the orphanage." He was anxious to see me, but the nanny dared not give him my address in the labor camp because I was still wearing the "cap." She believed that the authorities of the camp would not let him see me anyway. Thus the student was obliged to return home leaving behind one kilo of peanuts and half a kilo of sesame oil for the nanny to forward to me.

When I received the food, tears ran down my cheek. He seemed too young when he left the orphanage to remember so much. I did not expect that twenty-seven years later he would travel such a long way from Shandong to look for me time and again, bringing me food which was rarely seen in the markets and so disappointed every time when I was not found. Who was I to be so treasured by God? It was solely God's wonderful work to encourage me and strengthen my faith that I should live with hope and complete the last stage of my life on earth by His strength.

On August 18, the eighteenth day of my return home, I received a letter from a stranger. He introduced himself as a former student of *Shanghai Theological Seminary*. In his letter, he warned me to be aware of several matters. I will write down three points addressed in his letter and my answers to him:

1. "Don't forget the trouble after tasting its bitterness."

My answer was: "The Lord disciplines those He loves. The fact that I am disciplined proves that I am loved by God. Moreover, I believe that the imprisonment was a wonderful opportunity for me to practice the truth that I have learned because sufferings are good tools employed by the Lord to train His children so that they will be molded into a vessel suitable to His heart's desire."

2. "Now times are different and people have changed their hearts. The old experience is outdated."

My answer was: "A Christian who is willing to be guided by the Holy Spirit and boasts only in his Lord does not rely on his experience but on the gracious and truthful Lord and eternal God. He is always reliable, always faithful, and with Him, there is no shadow of turning. Although we fail, He is still faithful, because He cannot fail Himself. "Heaven and earth will pass away; the Word of the Lord will never pass away" (Luke 21:33).

3. "There are many false believers, and it is common practice to give up one's belief. For people to become lovers of themselves and never attentive to others' need is a popular phenomenon among Christians."

I answered: "That phenomenon is not unusual. Otherwise, what Paul mentioned in 2 Timothy
3:1-5 about there being people deviating from true
teachings would not be God breathed."

Unfortunately that former seminary student kept his
eyes on circumstances, on others and on himself. He was
like the prodigal son who left his father. He married the
widow of a nonbeliever and spent his daily life in quarrel-
ing. He thought that he could convince me by his knowledge and understanding, and that I would follow him. Was
he not too naive?

I appreciated his concern, however, I felt there was a
big problem with him in that he studied the Word of God
but did not practice it. A heavy-headed and weak-legged
person will certainly topple. He read the Bible, but did not
digest it. He was uncertain about God, which led him to a
halfhearted faith. When he met difficulty, he would think
that it was not worthwhile to suffer.

We are weak, and the only way to stand firm, to fight
and bear witness for the Lord is to keep close communion
with Jesus so that we will be strengthened spiritually. We
must be very clear about it. If we think that it is useless to rely
on God, we will fall because of lack of faith. We must trust
the Lord with all our hearts, obey the guidance of the Holy
Spirit, put on the full armor of God and take the sword of the
Spirit, which is the Word of God, to pray in all occasions.
Then we are "more than conquerors through Him who
loves us" (Romans 8:37).

In Shanghai, I received two letters from fellow prisoners, both nonbelievers. A woman more than sixty years
old wrote in her letter: "Remember how you suffered
during the days when the "Gang of Four" were riding wild

over the country. My heart was aching when the relentless blows fell upon you." Another woman was an intellectual over forty years old. She said, ". . . I shall forsake these (the sufferings she had undergone) which made me sad. I envy you, a pious Christian, your everlasting joy that will not be clouded by trouble or torture. Am I right? Please guide me because I am still in suffering. I pin all my hope together with my body and soul upon my husband. Will he be reliable when I am getting old? We love each other now. Shall I meet the fate of attracting nobody's love when I am getting old like a withered tree or a fallen flower? The unselfish love of parents has gone for good. Please guide me."

I did not agree with her that my joy was because of my piety. In reality, my everlasting joy resulted, not from my piety, but from my awareness of the great faithfulness, wisdom and sovereign power of my Lord. Why should I be anxious when I am protected by One who keeps me as the apple of His eye? His grace promises more than that. He has kept for me in heaven an inheritance that can never perish, spoil or fade. He not only gives me great hope, He fills my heart with joy and peace, spiritual power and grace.

When I first returned, my neighbors did not allow me to use the kitchen. They even threw my coal cake oven out of the kitchen. I reasoned with them in vain. They told me to ask for permission from the *Housing Administration Bureau* and Residents Committee. Whenever I was in difficulty, I would talk to the Lord who carried my burden every day. I did the same this time. However, my neighbors presented the complaint first and accused me before the Residents Committee that very night.

The next morning, at about seven, I went to the *Housing Administration Bureau* and was told that the kitchen should be shared. From there I went directly to the

Residents' Committee. Two cadres from the Committee then came over to our residence to assess the situation in the kitchen, and they finally demanded that my neighbors empty some space for me to put my stove. One of the neighbors invented some story about sister Huang and me to aggravate one of the cadres to criticize me. However, the other cadre criticized the neighbor for not allowing me to use the kitchen. Another neighbor was afraid of them and dared not utter a word. In the end the oven was placed in the kitchen.

Although the oven issue was settled, there was still no place for me to put a chair or a table to store my cooking utensils. The nanny who was taking care of my sister's grandson urged me to ask the Residents Committee to resolve the problem again. She was also worried about my living expenses because I had no income. She even told other believers that I had financial difficulty. What should I do when being urged time and again?

As a messenger of the Lord, should I keep relying on the Residents Committee to straighten things out for me? No, I could not do that. I believed that the Heavenly Father must arrange everything for me. With the help of the Holy Spirit I should emit the fragrance of Christ. It is my privilege to commit everything into the hands of my Heavenly Father and rely on Him to solve the problem.

God heard my prayer. A few days later, the bullying neighbor emptied some space for me of his own accord so that I could put in a small cabinet. If I had followed the advice of the nanny, it might have aroused hatred between us. Psalm 147:10-11 says: "His pleasure is not in the strength of the horse, nor his delight in the legs of a man; the Lord delights in those who fear him, who put their hope in his unfailing love."

I treated my neighbors kindly. Sometimes when I had some delicacy from brothers and sisters in Christ, I would share it with my neighbors. We became friends. When I had visitors and was not at home or did not hear their knocks, my neighbors would tell me. During the holidays when there was no one to buy groceries for me, my neighbor would offer to shop for me. Actually, those who are willing to humble themselves before the Lord will be exalted by Him.

Chapter 16

Blessings Undeserved

A motorcycle accident

Since I returned home, many people came to fellowship with me. Often my mind was distracted. Occasionally I would follow the flesh and think that I had in some degree helped myself to be released from the labor camp. Such thoughts should be rejected right away, even if they are rare. I should put the flesh to death all the time without leaving any room for it. I should be a "garden locked up, a spring enclosed and a fountain sealed" (Song of Songs 4:12), used solely by the Lord. Seeing how weak I was spiritually and knowing what I needed, the Lord who searches my heart allowed this incident.

The motorcycle accident happened on September 14, 1979, about seven weeks after I returned home. I was going to visit a friend from our camp who had written several times to invite me to her home. She said she would be at home after six in the evening. Because of my poor eyesight, I was afraid that I might not be able to distinguish the street numbers of her home easily in that late hour. I left my eldest sister's home at about 5:45 and hurried across the street, hoping to arrive at her home in time. The moment I crossed the street, a motorcycle traveling at full speed ran into me and broke my left leg.

At first, I did not know my leg was broken. I tried to stand up and walk, but was unable. I sat on the street with my left leg numb. Immediately, a young soldier came over to me. Seeing blood gushing from the broken leg, he stopped a truck and carried me onto it. He then accompanied me to the nearby *Huashan Hospital* and left before I could thank him. The hospital record only told me that I was handed to the nurses by a young soldier. It was a pity that he left before I could show my gratitude.

The doctors and nurses hurried to check my blood pressure. An x-ray of my left leg showed that my femur was fractured. The doctor put a cast on my leg and gave me several shots, but that did not stop the bleeding. During the emergency treatment, I felt no pain, but was thirsty and asked for water, which was readily given.

Later a traffic policeman came to the hospital to ask where I came from and where I was going. When he asked for my address, I gave him my eldest sister's address. When my sister learned about the incident, she hurried to send her granddaughter and a brother in Christ who was working in my sister's home as a carpenter.

The young man who rode the motorcycle also came to the hospital accompanied by the policeman. He brought me home by car at nine that evening. At the gate we met two women vendors whom I did not know. They voluntarily carried me from the car up to my room on the third floor through several winding staircases. The young man visited me often. He also invited his relatives to come to see me. Every time they came they brought me powdered milk and fruit. I tried to persuade them not to bring presents but without success. I took every opportunity when they visited me to preach the gospel.

One day, a coworker of that young man asked me, "Did you believe in Jesus because you suffered from certain heavy blows?" I told him that I received Jesus not because of any heavy blow, but had been following Jesus from childhood, and my faith in Him had never changed. They were surprised at my words. It was just like what is written in 1 Corinthians 1:18: "For the message of the cross is foolishness to those who are perishing, but to us who are being saved it is the power of God."

The young man who caused that accident was once in the navy. After his mother died, he was assigned to work in the Customs House. He told me that he was very upset after he broke my leg, thinking that his whole life would be ruined by that accident. Usually the person responsible for a car accident has to pay an enormous sum of money for the medical bills and living expenses of the victim. That imposes a great burden on the person responsible, whose income may be limited. I did not ask for any compensation because I hoped that he would come to know the love of God and receive Jesus to be his Savior.

He was moved and repeated several times that he would not shirk his responsibility because of my kindness. Actually, he did his best to see that I had the proper treatment. Several times when he came with his friends, they carried me down from the third floor and transported me to the hospital for my medical checkups in a big van. Later the doctor added a plaster heel to my cast so I could move around in the room by myself.

When I was resting at home, the Lord gave me time to examine myself. He wanted me to surrender completely, to be gentle and lowly, and to obey Him absolutely. The Lord also moved some brothers and sisters in Christ to visit me from time to time. Early one morning, there came an unfamiliar elderly lady more than eighty years old. She said that she was going to visit a relative, but when she walked to the corner of the street, she was moved to visit me. She told me that she had been praying for me since I was in Shanghai Prison and took out two pieces of Beijing candies for me to show her goodwill. She said that during the Cultural Revolution she was hit by a car and broke her arm. When she was obliged to stay home, the Residents Committee held meetings to denounce the ministers working in the church. However, she was excused from attending those meetings because of her broken arm. She added that I could rest assured because the Lord must have a good plan for me. I was very comforted by her visit.

The Lord also moved other brothers and sisters to come and help me with domestic chores, some of whom I hardly knew. One day I received sister Ling who came from a district far away. She told me that she and her elder sister had been praying for me for over twelve years. Her sister passed away half a year ago. To fulfill her sister's wishes, she made this special trip to visit me in spite of her grief and her own delicate health. I deemed it a special blessing of God to be so loved by others.

The visits were a great encouragement. I became acutely aware that because these brothers and sisters prayed incessantly for me, our Almighty God eventually delivered me from my slavery in the labor camp. Furthermore, the Lord opened my eyes and let me know that if it were not for His special mercy I might have been killed or become a cripple. I should be grateful and praise Him that I was not injured in the head when my leg was broken.

Unexpected visitors

On November 9, 1979, I received some unexpected visitors: Dai-En Xu, my student in the orphanage, Xing-En Xu, his sister, and their mother and aunt. Their visit reminded me of a story thirty years earlier. In the spring of 1949, Dai-en Xu lost his father. Because of their poverty, mother Xu was obliged to send her three beloved children to our orphanage. The eldest was a very lovely and clever girl whom we named Ming-En. En means grace. Because she was found to have some kind of lung disease, possibly contagious to other children, I had to ask mother Xu to take her home. So Ming-En followed her mother to Hong Kong, where she was educated in a public school and worked in business after she finished her education.

For years, Ming-En and her mother kept looking for her brother, Dai-En, and her sister, Xing-En. She sent people to inquire from me about her brother's and sister's whereabouts twenty years ago, but I could give them no clue then because our orphanage had already merged with Bethany. This time, they wrote to a police station asking for help from the resident's registration policemen, who soon helped them find their addresses. Ming En made contact with her brother by phone. Then she prepared enough money for her mother and aunt to meet them in Shanghai. She also asked her mother to give me fifty yuan. Although Ming En did not stay in our orphanage for long, she still remembered me. How should I count the blessing of the Lord, who remembers everything we do for Him, whether it is done in secret or in public.

Our labor in the Lord is never in vain. Things I did for those little ones were remembered; how much more our other ministry. The Lord says, "I tell you the truth, whatever you did for one of the least of these brothers of mine, you did it for me" (Matthew 25:40).

The Bible also says, "Let us not become weary in doing good, for at the proper time we will reap a harvest if we do not give up" (Galatians 6:9). Actually I never expected that my students, from whom I was separated for thirty years, would remember their early life in the orphanage. How amazing are the deeds of the Lord!

I remember when I was arrested and detained in the branch of *Shanghai Security Bureau*, the Lord gave me a verse, "Call for me in the day of trouble, I will deliver you and you will glorify me" (Psalm 50:15).

Everything in the world has its own law of growth and development. This is also true of spiritual growth. God is the origin of wisdom and He knows everything in the future. He knows what is helpful to those whom He loves. He is willing to give us the best, but He waits until we are able to receive them.

The ideas, talents, strengths, cleverness, and craftiness of the self are all barriers to receiving gifts from God. Therefore, God must wait until we abandon all these by the power of the Holy Spirit and are willing to reject every natural desire and obey His will. Then He will give us without any delay what He has prepared for each of us, the greatest and most valuable that we can ever imagine.

God will reveal Himself to everyone who trusts and obeys Him with all his heart. His glory will be manifested upon him, and His will be done through him. Therefore I shall continue to let Him be the center of my life, to trust and obey Him with all my heart, with my eyes fixed upon Him until I finish my race on earth.

Justice to His servants

One day when I was resting in bed, a stranger from Fujian Province came to visit me, accompanied by an engineer who was working in Shanghai. That engineer told me a story about a pastor's wife in a church in Suzhou, whose husband used to be my coworker in Shanghai. During the Cultural Revolution, the pastor's wife tried to accuse a believer who truly loved the Lord to win favor from the authorities as someone they could trust.

In a political accusation meeting she also urged the wife of that engineer to charge that believer. When accusing the believer with all kinds of expressions, that pastor's wife was suddenly attacked by a stroke and half of her body was paralyzed. She has been in bed ever since. The story revealed to me once again that God must render justice for all the oppressed and work righteousness for the poor. Those who suffer from injustice should lift their case to the Lord without being angry or arguing with their oppressor.

The work of God must be manifested. Let all those who are persecuted for the sake of the Lord praise Him with joy. Even when we are rebuked or attacked for our own sin, we should not lose heart. Confess to the Lord and repent, then hand everything to the Lord. He forgives our sin and cleanses our iniquity.

Another grievous story happened in Kunming, Yunnan, in Southwest China. Sun S.X., an activist pastor of the Three-Self Church was rash and treacherous, using tricks and hoaxes to accuse his coworkers and denounce many faithful servants of the Lord. He would abuse his fellow workers and even occupy by force another minister's house which was well-structured, well-lighted and well-ventilated.

One day his daughter-in-law took his only grandson to visit him and they stayed overnight in the house he had occupied by force. In the night, a fire broke out killing his whole family, young and old. The minister who had been driven out of his home was safe and sound. Thus, his life and most of his wealth were still protected from above.

When Sun snatched personal gains by any means, he was proud of himself. Sometimes it seemed that God was not a righteous God. Some people even doubted God's existence. However, God stretched out His righteous hand at the time set by Him. "Your love, O Lord, reaches to the heavens, your faithfulness to the skies. Your righteousness is like the mighty mountains, your justice like the great deep" (Psalm 36:5-6).

From Marah to Elim

The pilgrimage of the children of God is not always pleasant. Sometimes they shall walk on a rough and winding mountain path, sometimes through dark forests with roaring animals, and sometimes in a boundless desert under a scorching sun. Then the presence of God seems so remote, no pillar of cloud and pillar of fire, no end of trouble. However, in the time of perplexity we shall grasp the promise of God, do what is pleasing in His sight, praise the Lord at His gate and lift our eyes to Him in prayer. We shall wait on God. He will lead us from Marah to Elim.

Four months passed since the motorcycle accident. The doctor of *Huashan Hospital* thought that the cast could be taken off, but the director of the department checked my leg and suggested that the cast stay on longer. I had to wait with patience.

A minister wrote letters to me and asked, "Why did God let you break your leg after He finally led you out of the labor farm?" As for me, that was not a question because it was my Father's good pleasure to let it happen, and every-thing arranged by Him is good.

One day I received a letter from Nanjing from sister Chen inviting me and my grandnephew to stay with her. Sister Chen came from a family of several generations of Christians. Her grandmother and mother were strong Christians. She had dedicated herself to the Lord when she was about eleven or twelve years old. Later she heard some exaggerated or invented propaganda in a political accusation meeting in the church, which turned her from God.

Fifteen years later, her family was attacked in the Cultural Revolution. The whole family was driven out of their home and lived in a funeral home. She suffered from cancer and was tormented by severe stomach pains. Under a series of heavy blows—hardship, illness, persecution—she revived spiritually. The Lord Himself worked in her family and led them back to His fold. Her sister-in-law and sisters prayed hard for her. She confessed her sin and repented, and her serious illness was healed by the Lord.

One day she read my autobiography, *A Living Testimony*, in Chinese and heard that I had returned from the labor camp. She urged her brother and sister-in-law to visit me. When they came, they expressed their hope that I would come for a rest in Nanjing. She also arranged school for my grandnephew and asked sister Lee Lian Dexun to arrange everything for me.

Sister Lee was a medical worker and mother of three children. To enable me to go to Nanjing, she came to my home early in the morning by bicycle to help me settle various affairs. Showers of God's great love fell upon me. Helped by brothers and sisters in Christ, we took the train and arrived in Nanjing, my "Elim."

The Lord prepared an unfamiliar peasant to carry me from the train at Nanjing station and place our luggage on the platform. Sister Chen, her sister-in-law and another brother were waiting for us. Sitting on her bicycle, I was carried from the station. Then they took us on a bus, and again on a bicycle to her home.

The following day, Sister Chen carried me on her bicycle to the hospital for an x-ray. The doctor found that my femur bone had not healed well, but it was too late to do anything about it, and my cast was removed. At first, walking was awkward. Sister Chen bought some Chinese medicine from the hospital to wash my leg. She was very attentive and considerate in taking care of me and providing needed rest for me in the quietness of her home. I was so blessed by the Lord, as Psalm 41:3 says, "The Lord will sustain him on his sickbed and restore him from his bed of illness."

One day an unfamiliar young sister came and gave me five yuan. These were saved from her transportation fee, which she was willing to offer to the Lord. I felt that I did not deserve such an offering, which was as precious as the two coins offered by the poor widow mentioned by Jesus. With a heart of gratitude, I sent the money to an old sister who had suffered for many years for the Lord in the labor camp.

A few days later, another young sister offered me three yuan, which was her scholarship. I saw that she was very weak physically and felt that I did not deserve that offering so I sent it again to that old sister who was in greater need.

God also encouraged and helped me to grow in faith by leading sinners to Himself. One early Sunday morning after personal devotions, we folded the two beds in our room and arranged several benches for the worship service. Among those who attended the service was a strong young man. We talked with him after the service and learned that

he studied in an agriculture college. His aunt was a professor in a university in America and a very pious Christian.

The young man announced at the beginning of our
conversation, "I do not believe in God, and no one can
compel me to believe in Him. I will not believe in God unless
I know it for sure." I told him to rest assured that I would not
compel anyone to believe. Then I told him about God's
creation, the belief in God of the great scientist Edison, the
sin of man, and the death and resurrection of Jesus Christ.

The second time he came, he was humbler and the
air of pride and presumption disappeared. That day I told
him, "It is impossible to know God thoroughly. For example, there is a hungry man who has some food in front of
him which he can eat. If he believes that food cannot meet
his hunger until he has learned all about biology, he will die
of hunger. It is the same in receiving Jesus as one's Savior.
One need not wait until he completely knows God. All he
has to do is confess his sin and receive Jesus as his Savior. If
he is willing, the Holy Spirit opens his heart and lets him
know God and His great and amazing deeds." That day he
said that he was standing at the gate of salvation but had not
yet entered. Later I told him the importance of entering the
door.

On Easter Day, we each drew a verse of God's
promise. The verse the young man drew was John 4:24,
"God is spirit, and His worshipers must worship in spirit and
in truth." When each of us read our verses in turn, he stood
up and said that the verse spoke to him. Praise the Lord, he
entered the door of salvation. After I left, I was told that he
even led his fellow students to worship God. All this was the
result of the work of the Holy Spirit, because "When he
comes, He will convict the world of guilt in regard to sin and
righteousness and judgment" (John 16:8).

A few days later I was surprised by some very good

news. I heard someone talking with Sister Chen about something in Qinghai. That person mentioned the name of Du Hengwei, which caught my attention. I longed to know things about the brothers and sisters in Xining, Qinghai. It was a surprise to hear their news in Nanjing.

Who was speaking? He was a brother from Qinghai. He said that Du Hengwei was rehabilitated, that the elder was released, and that the believers in that area had experienced spiritual revival and the number of believers had increased. The fact that some Christians were killed like James and some released like Peter does not suggest that the released were more mature spiritually than those who were killed. God has different plans for different people. Many things we do not understand now, but we will understand when we see God.

I am reminded that many missionaries from the Western countries left their beloved families and friends and their comfortable homes to come to China after several months of ocean voyage. They wanted the light of the gospel to shine in our dark land, a land full of superstition and idols. They even gave their lives and shed their blood on this foreign land for the sake of the gospel.

In the years of 1900 and 1901, 136 missionaries and 53 children of missionaries, totaling 189 people, were killed for the Lord. Now Sister Du Hengwei followed them to die a martyr's death. However, God will never be defeated. He will continue to raise His faithful servants to lead His lost sheep back to His sheep fold. He will manifest His sovereign power and make His name known to all nations. Almighty God, may you receive my praise and worship!

Young brother from overseas

Unexpectedly, a young brother who was the son of the very devoted sister, Mrs. Hsu Lin Yutang, whom I knew forty-three years before, came from Japan and wanted to visit me. He asked someone to look for my address beforehand and informed me that he would come from Beijing to Nanjing to visit me. At that good news, my heart bowed down before God, and my spirit was filled with praise for His amazing guidance.

On July 19 the young brother came. He was brave and clever, quiet and firm, humble and very loving. He told me that his mother had urged him to see me, saying that he should not forget the good he had received. Although I did not talk much with him, I knew that he was very concerned about the family of God and was willing to find possible solutions for all the problems.

Although only in his twenties, he was already in charge of an Engineering Department for an overseas company. This time, he came to negotiate a cooperative project between the two countries. However, his main concern was the Lord's work.

When he returned, he wrote letters to me, asking me to visit his aunt and other relatives. I was moved by his fervor for the salvation of his relatives. Guided by the Holy Spirit, I went to see his aunt after I returned from Nanjing and talked with her about the salvation of God.

His aunt used to be a Christian, but she had been out of contact with other brothers and sisters in Christ for years. There was no one to guide her spiritually. By God's grace, when I visited her, she said that she needed Jesus to be her Savior. Not long after, she left the earth to be with her Father in Heaven. Her rest reminds me of the description of our life on earth in James 4:14: "You are a mist that appears for a little while and then vanishes."

Brother Hsu was truly a faithful servant of God. The fervor of his concern surpassed average believers and ministers. When he heard that my book *Living Testimony* was out-of-print, he decided immediately that he would reprint 1,000 copies in Japan at his own expense.

It was also commendable that he was serious about honoring his mother's request. Every time he came to Shanghai, he would squeeze time from his tight schedule to visit me. He would come suddenly and sit for a brief time, often five or ten minutes. Within that short time, I could find nothing to entertain him, not even a cup of tea, but he did not mind. Sometimes he would come right from the airport to visit me without having a meal. Usually, he would bring me some copies of the Bible and spiritual literature. He often got into trouble because of this.

One day, his Bibles and books were detained by the Customs House. He was indescribably distressed when he came to see me empty-handed. At that time the Bible was not freely available in China. He grieved for those whose spiritual hunger and thirst could not be fed. To love God and his neighbors he paid dearly, but he was persistent in doing good for the Lord without considering his own interest.

He came to Shanghai again in the evening before National Day. The whole city was under curfew, and there were no street lights in certain areas. He stayed at a hotel far from my home, but decided to walk to my home when he could not find any transportation. Fortunately, he met a taxi along the way so that he could finish his journey by car.

Another time when he came to Shanghai, the city was attacked by a hurricane. There was hail in the suburbs and in the Shanghai Bunds, through which he had to pass, and many electric poles had been blown down. Under such a situation he still managed to come to see me.

In my old three story building there lived more than a dozen families. Each family tried to occupy as much public space as possible. They even piled up miscellaneous things on both sides of the corridor, leaving a narrow path for only one person to pass through. However, no one took care of cleaning this space. Whenever I reached my lodging, somebody was there waiting to talk with me. So I could not find time to clean the staircases either.

One night after eleven when the whole neighborhood was in quiet sleep, Brother Hsu managed to fumble his way through all the barriers in the corridor and came up to my room on the third floor without a flashlight. I was so encouraged to see him beaming with a smile without any complaint. In the newspaper, we often read that some young people, even highly educated ones, treat their parents cruelly. In their eyes, aged parents are a waste. What Brother Hsu did for me for the love of the Lord will be remembered!

Jesus says, "No one who has left home or brothers or sisters or mother or father or children or fields for me and the gospel will fail to receive a hundred times as much in this present age, homes, brothers, sisters, mothers, children and fields—and with them, persecutions, and in the age to come, eternal life" (Mark 10:29-30).

The concern and supply extended to me by Brother Hsu were far beyond what many parents receive from their own children. He not only treated me kindly, but rendered excellent care to many other servants of God and aged people, which he did in secret without leaving his name. May all glory be to our Sovereign God.

Cousin from abroad

The Lord, my Heavenly Father, brought me exciting good news. When I returned from Nanjing in July 1980, I received a letter from my cousin, Wang Chou Che-chin saying that she would be coming to China in September. I remember when we studied together in the same school when she was a teenager, and how we went together to our aunt's home to preach the gospel. She became a nurse, then was married and moved to Taiwan. We lost contact for many years.

In her letter, she told me that she was now living in America and her children were all working there. She missed her relatives in China and wanted to visit us. We had been separated for thirty-six years. I never dreamed that we would ever meet again.

She brought me many things for my physical and spiritual need. It made me happy to know that she and her husband were Christians. Her son served the youth in the church as a volunteer. Her youngest daughter, also a Christian, was studying and working part-time.

After a few days rest in Shanghai, we went together to our aunt's home in the countryside to visit the tomb of our uncle. It was a pity that our relatives were concerned more about material things than the eternal blessing—to receive Jesus Christ as their Savior. We stayed in the countryside for a few days. To settle some odd jobs at home, I returned first to Shanghai.

Several months later, I invited a sister in Christ to witness to my aunt. She eventually received Jesus as her Savior, even refusing to eat the food that her daughter-in-law prepared because it had been sacrificed to idols during Chinese New Year.

Revised verdict

On October 13, not long after returning from Nanjing, I received a notice from the Residents Committee informing me to go to court the following morning at nine. I remembered that the judge told me, "It was and is still forbidden to translate religious books, as well as to hold family worship," when my case was reviewed in June. I replied, "Please stipulate clearly what is allowed and what is prohibited. Different people have different views and one does not know whom to follow." This time, the court was supposed to give me a formal reply.

That evening I met Brother Hsu and he volunteered to accompany me to the Hongkou District People's Court by car the following morning. There I received this revised verdict:

> Shanghai Hongkou District People's Court Criminal Verdict (63) HCVR 145
> Petitioner Wang Chunyi, female, 65 years old, living at 365 Ermei Road, Shanghai.
>
> Due to an anti-revolutionary case, Wang Chunyi was sentenced to ten years imprisonment in Criminal Verdict (63) HCR 145 by above mentioned court on November 20, 1963. The above petitioner was not convinced by the original verdict and appealed for. . . . The director of above mentioned court found that there are mistakes both in confirming facts and applying law for the verdict which is proposed to the Arbitration Committee. After discussion, the Arbitration Committee decided to reexamine the case.
>
> The findings of the review of the court are as follows: Wang Chunyi is a Christian, and the fact that she translated *The Prayer Life*, compiled the small tract *Rise and Pray*, and held family worship service does not form a crime. The original verdict which sentenced her to the crime of anti-revolutionary was obviously improper. Therefore, it is decided:
> (1) Repeal the decision of Verdict (63) HCA 145
> (2) Declare the innocence of Wang Chunyi

If the petitioner is not convinced by the present verdict, she can re-appeal to the Shanghai Middle People's Court within ten days starting from the following day she received the verdict.

> Chief Judge: Desou Ma
> Judge: Huoming Chou
> Deputy Judge: Phoning Gu
> Recorder: Yifong Shen
> October 14, 1980

The court made several copies of the verdict and sent them to the *Public Security Bureau*. God also guided a very capable and godly brother to help me make several copies of the verdict. I was very happy to receive the verdict and especially to know that the authorities concerned had admitted their mistake in labeling *The Prayer Life* and *Rise and Pray* as poisoned literature and had announced that holding family services did not constitute a crime.

Abundant Grace

I had a student in the orphanage who was imprisoned because she applied to open a church and possessed a copy of *The Prayer Life*. In the labor camp, she prayed for the healing of an authority's sick wife. God answered her prayer and healed the woman. Thus, she was released before the completion of her sentence.

One day, a brother who was familiar with that student came to see me. When he learned about the revised verdict of my case, he made a copy of it and sent it to that student. It was very helpful for her to have that copy. The policeman in charge of the village where she lived copied the contents of my verdict so it is now known that *The Prayer Life* was purely related to the truth of Christianity and had no political motives. Thus, they could no longer attack Christian literature willfully.

By God's grace some known brothers and sisters came to comfort me and have fellowship with me. Some came because they had read my book, *The Living Testimony*. After I was arrested, the workers in the Residents Committee set up big posters announcing that I had a transmitter and contacted an enemy radio station in secret to deceive the residents in the neighborhood. Workers of the Three-Self Church also made up some stories about me to deceive the believers in the Hongkou Church. However, in due time all the false accusations collapsed like houses built on sand.

Everyone who is able to think will know that falsehood will eventually be seen through. The Bible says, "There is nothing concealed that will not be disclosed, or hidden that will not be made known" (Matthew 10:26). If one wants to achieve his ulterior motive by cheating, he will be like those who pick up a stone to throw at others, but hurt themselves. I did not lose brothers and sisters in Christ because of false attacks against me. On the contrary, people who came and showed their concern to me were even more devoted than before I was arrested.

One day a minister's daughter said to me, "After the Cultural Revolution, our family was very weak spiritually. When we read *The Living Testimony*, we all cried and our faith was strengthened."

Some people came with problems, hoping I could help them. Foolish as I am, I relied on the merciful God to give them their answers. Others came with prayer requests. Sometimes, I felt I did not have enough energy to meet their needs.

For quite a long time, I had to cook my meals on a coal stove, but with a deteriorating memory, I often forgot the food cooking on the stove when talking with the visitors.

Sometimes the food burned, or when I forgot to add a coal cake, the fire would go out. It was not rare for me to delay lunch until two in the afternoon.

Often after my visitors had left, I had to listen to the endless complaints of one of my neighbors. She and her husband received more labor security payments than average persons, yet she tended to see the dark side of everything. All I could do was tell her to rely on the Lord Jesus who was the author and perfecter of our faith.

Some people came to see me as early as five in the morning; others stopped late at night when I had already turned off my light. When the conversation got too long, I would be so sleepy that I had to make an effort to keep my eyes open. I prayed for help to overcome my fatigue. Then God moved Mrs. Hsu LiuYutang to send me some nourishing medicine from abroad, which increased my energy to continue my ministry among the visitors.

My dentist told me that he should pull all my remaining teeth and make a set of dentures for me. It was a surprise when sister Li, a teacher in my high school, sent me sixty yuan from Hong Kong for the dental fee.

Later I heard that sister Chiu Sun-Lingli, wife of Pastor Stephen Chiu, was asking about my whereabouts. Mrs. Chiu was a very devoted sister, born into a family of an industrial proprietor. Her father loved the Lord. When he was the boss of a factory, he would let his workers rest and worship God on Sundays with the same pay as they received on weekdays. After her graduation from college, Lingli went to work in our orphanage for a while. She was neither proud nor spoiled, and was very firm in her faith. When she did something wrong, she would admit her fault. She deeply loved the orphans and was very considerate of her coworkers. In any case, she did not lose her smile nor utter a word of complaint.

While working in the orphanage, she was called by the Lord to enter the *Ministers College* for further spiritual formation. She then married a faithful servant of God, Pastor Stephen Chiu, a graduate of *Fudan University* and *China Theological Seminary*. They served the Lord with one mind and remained faithful with great courage in the face of hardship, misery, and sickness.

Mrs. Chiu often gave away what she received from the Lord. She even saved from her own budget to help other coworkers. Often she was quietly doing something other people did not want to do or which was neglected by others. She suffered from a heart condition for which she received surgical treatment in America with a good prognosis. As soon as she got better, she continued to work for the Lord day and night.

She eventually assisted Pastor Chiu in planting a Chinese church in Boston, Massachusetts and the number of believers grew from a dozen to more than three hundred. To meet the needs in Southeast Asia, they decided to leave the United States and go serve there. They left a very good example for the believers to follow.

A believer who had been in difficulty wrote to me, saying, "The day before Pastor and Mrs. Chiu's departure, they hurried to my home to show me their concern, comfort and encouragement, which I will never forget in my life." When Mrs. Chiu heard that I was released, she immediately sent me money she had put aside for me.

Sister Li Liang Singde was also one who showed me great concern. Although she was extremely busy, she thought about everything that I would need at home and provided me with an iron bed, quilted bedding, pillow cases, etc. Those lovely sisters and their moving deeds filled my heart with joy.

Another sister, Mrs. Chen, a volunteer in the orphanage, came to see me and invited me to have fellowship with some other believers in her home. There I met several middle-aged visitors who had been students in the Sunday School class taught by Du Hengwei. They had gone down a winding path, even lost their faith, but they eventually returned to the shelter of their Heavenly Father. Praise the Lord for leading them back home.

I still remember them as children. Now their children were older than they had been. When they saw me, they told me earnestly that they were fooled by other people. They had doubted the truth and even lost their faith. They became friends of the world and endeavored to dig a pool that could not retain water. However, the result of all their efforts was misery and disappointment. While hurting others, they also hurt themselves. Fortunately, they returned to the truth that they believed in their childhood, which they recognized as the only way to deliver them. Their faith was restored and strengthened.

One of the sisters had a brother who was very concerned about other people's spiritual needs. When he found out that I had returned from the labor camp, he gave me an English Bible. Now that brother has dedicated himself to the Lord to preach the gospel and God has made him a channel for His grace.

They have let me see that if we sow by faith, we will reap in due time. Truly, it is more valuable than accumulating many material things, vain glory and high position. It is like what Jesus says, "Yet I tell you that not even Solomon in all his splendor was dressed like one of these" (Matthew 6:29).

Prayer and temptation

One day at an elderly lady's home I met a devoted sister who had been a Christian for many years. We were happy to meet again. Her first words were, "I have prayed for you every day." I asked, "What have you prayed for me?" She said, "For your health." I promptly asked her to pray for my spiritual life so that I would become a holy and useful instrument of the Lord. I believed that my spiritual life was more important than physical health.

Usually we are very concerned about physical illness or weakness and ignore the needs and growth of our spiritual life. When we are weak spiritually, we do not realize why. We neglect seeking the enlightenment of the Holy Spirit. We do not take the Word of God as our daily bread and prayer as our breath. Even when we pray, our prayer does not come from a pure heart. We may have some thoughts, hobbies or habits, which although not evil, tend to weary us spiritually. When these become an obstacle to our spiritual growth, we shall root them out by the power of the Holy Spirit. Then our spiritual life can grow and the image of Christ can be revealed in us.

There was a woman who often came to see me around seven in the morning. I was not certain whether she was sent by someone. From her conversation I knew that she was concerned about worldly power and glory instead of seeking faith and love in Christ, spiritual growth and God's will.

She often told me, "I pray for you every day. I pray that God will give you a position." Having sensed something wrong about that, I then asked, "What kind of position?" She said, "I pray that God will give you a position in the church. Then you can have a job with a stable income to secure your life." "Position," "job," "secure life"—these were all that she could think of.

I appreciated her concern for me, of course. However, I could not take a position as a minister to meet my needs in a church which was headed by false Christians or non-Christians.

I could not for the sake of physical needs or personal gain or reputation follow those who damaged the ministry of the gospel or confused the truth under the guise of Christianity. If I did so, I would befriend the world in the name of serving the Lord and lose my purity, my faith, my love and my loyalty to Him. I could even become an enemy of God.

That was why I rejected Rev. Peter Wang when he invited me to work in the Bible College. I am redeemed by the blood of Jesus and have become a member of the church. The church, the dwelling place of God through the Holy Spirit, is the body of Christ. Therefore, we shall seek the guidance of the Holy Spirit in every ministry in the church and obey the truth as it is written in Acts 13:1-3.

I shall do everything in Him who is the head, to unite with other members by Him in His love, and to serve Him with holiness and righteousness by the Holy Spirit. In addition, to honor the Word of God, to please Him and glorify Him, I will spread the good news to lost sinners that they will be saved. When I seek first His kingdom and His righteousness, God must satisfy all my needs. As to where or how to serve Him, I completely yield myself to Him for guidance.

So I told the woman who often came early in the morning, "I have a job." She asked, "What is your job?" I said that praying was my job, with God as my Master. And if He gave me dried turnips, the food of the poorest people, I would gladly receive it. I knew my God was faithful to provide all my needs.

Later I told the woman, "The prayer I need is that

God would help me to be a wise woman, instead of being a foolish one; to be a person of good understanding, not a muddle-headed one; to be filled by the Holy Spirit, not to be drunk, intoxicated by material things." Then the woman asked me to write down that prayer request, which I did. She never came back.

Besides those who claimed that they were praying for me, there were some other people who pretended to come for truth or fellowship, but whose real purpose was to spy on me. One morning, a choir member of a certain church came. She said that she wanted to have fellowship with me. Actually she was observing what I was doing at home and with whom I was in contact. She also wanted to know if I had any literature from abroad and asked for my testimony which I wrote after I was released from the labor camp.

One afternoon, when I went to meet a woman who was not a Christian yet, that choir member came. She brought a bottle of sesame oil and left it with a sister in my absence. At that time, sesame oil was a very expensive, edible oil and rarely available. When I learned about it, I told the sister to be cautious and not to receive gifts without thought.

Fortunately, that choir member returned the following day. I promptly gave the bottle of oil back to her. She said that she was moved by the Lord to give that bottle of oil to me. I told her that I was not moved by the Lord to receive it; besides I did not need it. She said that she no longer went to church and insisted that I was very godly because I did not attend church services. Many Christians did not join the church but worshiped God at home instead because believers did not want to be associated with the Three-Self Church. I told her that it was not a sign of godly people not to go to the churches. She was very surprised. Finally she left with that bottle of oil and never came back.

One evening, a Three-Self official made an open report about the situation of the churches in the country-side. He specially mentioned a woman minister who had studied in my orphanage. She later entered a minister's school for further education. Afterwards she went out to the countryside and worked with the churches there. To cheat believers and block their freedom to preach the gospel, the official accused the woman of several crimes she did not commit. Finally, he added in an insulting tone that the minister had been educated in our *Morning Star Orphanage*.

His true purpose was to scare people enough so that they dared not keep in contact with me or to frighten me so that I would refrain from serving the Lord. When the woman minister was in trouble for the third time, which I did not know at first, I found that my friendly neighbors became as strangers to me. Whenever I came in or went out, they would watch what I carried. However, the Lord gave me strength to remain calm. I was perfectly safe under His wings while more and more people still came to fellowship with me.

Then there came a woman dressed like an overseas Chinese, with whom I was not familiar. She was recommended by an American professor to have fellowship with me. She talked very friendly with me and invited me to stay in her house. She told me that I could play her piano and that she had a private telephone. At that time only people of high positions or having income in foreign currency were allowed to install telephones at home in China. She also told me that she had undergone much trouble during the Cultural Revolution. We started talking at four in the afternoon and did not finish our conversation until seven in the evening.

Because I did not know that woman, I prayed in secret for help the entire time while talking with her. If she really had a heart to seek God, I prayed that I would not offend her. If she had some ulterior motive, I prayed that I would not be fooled by her. I prayed hard in my heart that the Lord would open my spiritual eyes so that I would have divine wisdom and know how to talk with her.

A pastor had told me that she was a decent woman. But no matter what I heard from other people, my mind still focused on the Lord, waiting for Him to reveal to me His will. When the woman departed from me, the word, "Gibeonite," appeared repeatedly in my heart, a word that I was not even thinking about at the moment. So after I returned home, I asked other members in Christ to pray with me for further guidance.

Gradually God let me see clearly that she was a deceiver. With God's help, I learned that she had cheated a brother in Christ out of 8,000 Hong Kong dollars, some electric appliances and religious literature. She even secretly found out the list of friends with whom he associated which caused his detention and interrogation by the government for many days.

That woman also wanted to deceive me. Praise the Lord that He helped me to resist the temptation of seeking comfort in her home. Thus the Lord guarded me and all the people who had fellowship with me from getting into endless trouble.

As the hound is reluctant to give up the game it was chasing, Satan is unwilling to let go of those who serve the Lord. I have been threatened even when I was walking in the street. Whenever I encountered Satan's attacks, I would tell Jesus and He would calm me down with a Word from the Bible. One day He told me, "Great is our Lord and mighty in power; His understanding has no limit" (Psalm

147:5). Therefore, God reminded me that I trusted in the One who was mighty in power. And I should not be afraid of the people who must die.

God also taught me that He allowed all things for my good and that no trouble would come to me without His goodwill. He made me understand that when a farmer plowed for planting, he did not plow continually. Also, caraway was not threshed with a sledge, nor was a cartwheel rolled over cumin, but caraway was beaten out with a rod, and cumin with a stick, as written in Isaiah 28:24-27. Why should I lay on my shoulders a burden which was not necessarily to be carried by myself, since I trusted in a Lord of discretion?

Although lures and temptations came from all directions, I continued my pilgrimage with patience through the Lord. Eventually, temptations lose their attraction one after another, and children of God become more than conquerors through their triumphant Commander. This is the path of joy. The further one walks in the path, the lighter are his steps and the stronger he becomes. By the power of the Holy Spirit, the people of God will soar on wings like eagles and fly over deserts and cross oceans. How secure and how blessed it is to be God's people.

Better house provided

A diamond has a variety of beauty and color when it is viewed from different angles. So has the grace of God. We often think that it is God's grace to have a prosperous enterprise or robust health. Actually, it is also God's grace that we sometimes have hardship and sickness, which are used by Him to take care of His children and deliver them from greater temptation and danger. In our affliction, God speaks to us that we will know our path and ministry ahead.

There were twelve families living in our house. Each family used a coal cake stove with no chimney attached to it. Therefore the whole building was pervaded with gas from the stoves. In the cold winter, I caught the flu which caused an attack of laryngitis and constant coughing. Because of the toxic gas in the air, my coughing spells could not be suppressed by medicine.

Since there was no way to improve the ventilation, my coughing could not be stopped. Later I suffered from bursitis of the shoulder. I had sore shoulders and could not lift my arms. I took all sorts of medicine and received many shots, as well as massage therapy, but none gave me any relief.

Shortly after, my brother-in-law passed away and my sister was lonely, so I went to live with her for some time. During that period, I returned to my lodging three times a week to meet the needs of some brothers and sisters in Christ. One morning when I entered my room, I suddenly discovered that the lock on my door had been broken and there were traces of burglary on the door. However, I was surprised to find nothing missing—clothes, bedding and other daily necessities were all still there.

When sister Li heard about the incident, she offered for me to stay in her empty house free of charge. Her house was well located in a quiet corner of a busy neighborhood and it was very convenient to take city buses from her house. The rooms were well lighted by sunlight. There was also a private kitchen with a sanitary gas stove. In the densely populated city of Shanghai, where the average housing space for a resident was four square meters, with many families of three generations living in one room of the size of about twelve square meters, the chance to find such a comfortable house for me alone was as rare as finding a needle in a haystack. Besides, people would not know that

I had moved to a new house, so they could not come to see me.

God arranged everything so well for me. Now I could not only enjoy a sound rest but could avoid many dangerous traps. In my sickness and need, the Lord hid me in the shelter of His tabernacle and made me walk safely in high places. Is it not the amazing grace of God?

Chapter 17

Showers After the Long Drought

A word from the Lord

I mentioned in an earlier chapter that early in my ministry I went to preach in the countryside. Thirty years passed and the brothers and sisters there still remembered me, an undeserved maiden of God's grace. They often inquired from every possible source about how things stood with me. When they heard that I had returned from prison and the labor camp, they sent a brother to visit me.

It was a dark night when he arrived at my home. The hope of many years for us to have spiritual fellowship turned into reality. How shall we not be encouraged to see that the dark night will eventually be gone and broad daylight will shine brightly? The brother invited me to go to the countryside to his village and study the Bible with the brothers and sisters there. He did not know that I was still being monitored in secret although I was rehabilitated officially.

Outside the door of my room there was a water tap. Whenever my next door neighbors heard me talking with another in my room, they would go out immediately and start washing at the tap. They would stand beside the tap and keep on washing until my visitor left. After they saw my visitor, they would return to their own room. Every time I had a visitor, they would do the same thing. However, I was not afraid of being monitored because I knew that I was a child of Almighty God and under His care.

As to whether I should go to the countryside, I decided not to act before I knew God's will. So I did not give him a definite reply. Several months later, other people from the countryside came to visit me again, still hoping that I would visit them. I knew that "Go to the countryside" was God's will when I first dedicated myself to the ministry of the gospel, especially during the Anti-Japanese War. However, since that time, I worked mostly in the cities. Now I was being invited to work for the Lord in the countryside again. Why should I be so hesitant? How foolish I was! Thank God He gave me another opportunity to obey and go..

One day when I was living in an elderly sister's home, I was struck with a verse from the Bible, "Cursed are those who are idle from working for the Lord." That verse which I never thought of was lingering in my mind so that I could find no peace until I was willing to follow God's guidance completely without excuse or consideration for my safety.

The Chinese New Year was near at hand. On New Year's Eve, another brother came to tell me that his daughter would be married on the first day of Chinese New Year and he invited me to attend the wedding. That brother dared not admit that he was a Christian and had stopped attending worship services during the Cultural Revolution. Later he suffered from esophagus cancer and was unable to eat. When he was near death, his whole family repented and confessed their sins. With bitter tears, they returned to their Heavenly Father. God was merciful. He heard their prayer and healed him. Through his sickness he experienced the love and power of his Savior, so he dedicated himself and his whole family to the Lord. They started to hold family worship at home in spite of the persecution of the government.

Longing for God's Word

When I finally arrived in the countryside, we began our service the same evening. Their living room was filled with an eager audience. At seven we started the service with singing. At eight we began to share the Word of God, which was followed by Bible study and preaching. It was after nine when the service was finished. However, some brothers said that the time for the message was too short and that the service for the following day should be longer.

The next evening the service did not come to an end until well after ten. Still they thought the service was too short. Thus, they extended the service every evening. It was after midnight when the service closed on the last evening. Then some brothers and sisters came to me with some questions, which I tried my best to answer. We did not go to bed until about two in the morning.

Among the audience there were eight people who walked several hundred miles to attend the meetings. Only one sister among the eight had been a Christian for a long time. The rest were newly converted believers. Among them there was a young man who had been possessed by demons. Like the demon-possessed man in Jesus' time, he had been chained by his family members, but he tore the chains apart and no one was strong enough to subdue him. Praise the Lord, he was completely freed by believing in Jesus. Since then he pursued the truth. For that group of believers, it was a shower after a long drought to be able to attend the Bible study.

One day, a stranger came. He had seen me in the special New Spring Conference thirty years before when he was only a teenager. When he was told by some believers that I was staying in a certain brother's home, he hurried to look for me. At the sight of me, he burst into tears. It was the first time in my life I saw a middle-aged man cry so bitterly. He begged me to share the grace of the Lord at the church in his native village.

There was a special New Spring gathering of several hundred people in his church at the time. He urged me to preach the gospel there. I was moved by his fervor and sincerity. I would have gone with him if it were not for a woman minister in his church who had denounced many ministers. Some brothers, being concerned about my safety, rejected the idea that I should go share the truth there. Since I was not clear about God's guidance, I decided not to go this time.

Half a year later the brother came to visit me again. He did not know my address in Shanghai, but he took the risk to seek me by boat. On the boat he met another brother who knew my address and who was also going to invite me to speak in their gathering during the Chinese New Year. So they both came together to my home.

After much discussion, we thought that the church of the brother who wept bitterly had a greater need. We decided that I should first go to his church and then to the other brother's home. In the meantime, I asked the woman minister who had framed many people to send me an invitation. That way she could not denounce me later to the *Religious Administration Bureau*. Indeed, God heard their prayers and saw their bitter tears.

The church, which could seat over 600 people, was overcrowded in every service during the next several days. After I finished my service there, I went to serve in another village. Then God opened two more doors for me to preach the gospel. Praise the Lord that the grace of God came to every place I went. How eager were these brothers and sisters in the countryside for the truth, and their hunger for righteousness was beyond description.

At the gatherings I met a Communist Party member. His wife had suffered from an incurable disease and fully recovered after they converted to the Lord. There I also met a young man whose mother was a paralytic, and her condition failed to respond to any available medical treatment. Then someone told them about Jesus. They repented, confessed their sin and received Jesus as their Savior.

God heard their prayer, and the paralytic mother could now begin to move the upper parts of her body. However, her two legs still could not function. The brother who prayed for her asked her to examine her heart. She took out a shrine for idols and the ancestral tablets which she hid in the wall and burned them. Immediately she got out of her bed and began walking. The Holy and Jealous God does not want His children to hide their sin. He wants us to be holy and spotless.

Everywhere, the Holy Spirit proved the truth we preached with miraculous signs and wonders. Like bamboo shoots after rain, people who believed in the Lord were too numerous to count. Many new believers dedicated themselves to serve the Lord. Many went to preach the gospel in their spare time.

All praise, glory, and thanks be to our Triumphant King, who is far above all! Amen! ✹

Epilogue

Our God is the God of impossibilities. After I was released from the labor farm in China, I wrote this testimony in Chinese while in Nanjing, and sister Li copied it for me. The Lord blessed this work and the manuscript was taken out of China. My friend, brother Hsu, sent it to Mr. and Mrs. Tseng in the United States. I instructed them not to print it until after my death. However, it was printed in 1984 and sold in book stores.

Out of their concern for my safety, they changed the names. However, I felt that the names should not have been changed, and I tried to stop the sale of the books, but in vain. Brother Tung suggested that I should have the book reprinted. I felt that I was too old at seventy-two and my English was all but forgotten.

Moreover, it was not easy to apply for my passport and visa to leave China. I spent some time seeking God's will. The Lord showed me from Isaiah 54:2 that He did not want me to limit His way of doing things. I prayed that the Lord would confirm His will by sending me a letter from someone mentioning my going abroad.

Unexpectedly, Rev. Frank Wuest sent me a letter via Japan and asked me whether I planned to visit Canada. The Lord also sent me an invitation through my cousin's son, Ti-mai Wang. During my time of waiting before the Lord, He gave me this promise: "The steps of a good man are ordered by the Lord and He delighteth in his ways." The Lord began this work and He also performed it.

Suddenly the police department put a notice in the newspaper that whoever wanted to go abroad could now do so by applying for a passport. There was no limitation! However, at that time the American Consulate was especially strict in issuing visas. One famous writer was turned down in spite of having an invitation from a book store. One preacher who had close relatives in the United States was also turned down. However, when the Lord opens the door, no one can shut it. The day I went to the Consulate many students were refused visas and only three were approved. I was one of them.

September 27th, 1986, brother Hsu bought a ticket for me and I left for the United States via Hong Kong, where the Lord gave me opportunities to witness for Him in different churches. The day after I arrived in my cousin's home in Los Angeles, the leader of the Chinese Christian Church was a guest of my cousin's neighbor. When he heard about me, he invited me to give my witness in his congregation. I worked in his church for one year until I came to serve in the *Bread of Life Church.*

At the end of 1986, Mr. and Mrs. Ruey Chen sent me an air ticket from Washington, D.C. to attend the special missions conference of *Ambassadors For Christ, Inc.* There I met Dr. James Taylor III. We had good fellowship together, and he said he hoped I would attend his meeting when he came to Los Angeles in January 1987. When I returned from the East Coast, the Lord worked another miracle on my behalf. Miss Elizabeth Lowe, whom I had not met before, came to visit my roommate one evening. My roommate mentioned that I wished to go to hear Dr. Taylor's message. Immediately she took me from Monterey Park to the *Bread of Life Church* in Torrance. There the Lord arranged for me to meet Elder Ting, whom I also had not known before, and our Almighty God has given me the opportunity to serve in that church from 1988 until the present.

The Chinese edition of this testimony which was titled *Amazing!* was reprinted twice. My first book, *The*

256

Living Testimony, was also published in an English edition titled *His Mighty Power.* May God use these books to bring souls to Himself. I pray that many will surrender their lives to our precious Lord who is worthy to be praised and adored forever.

Esther Chunyi Wang